THE SHAW MEMORIAL

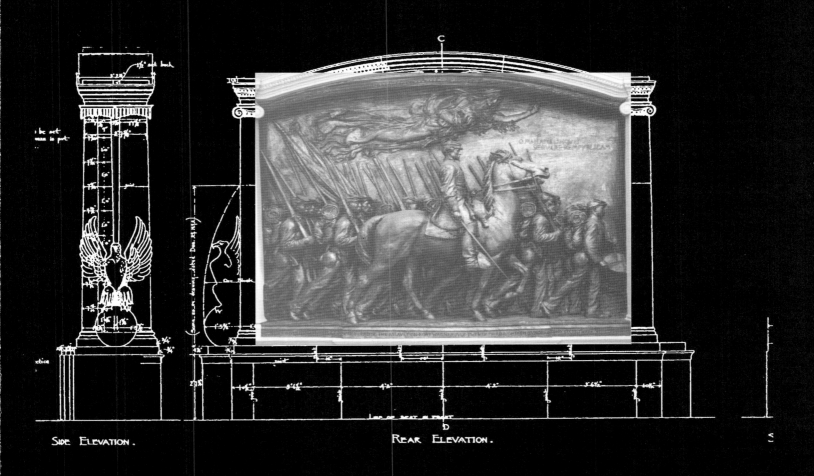

SIDE ELEVATION.   REAR ELEVATION.   S

A CELEBRATION OF
AN AMERICAN MASTERPIECE

Published by Eastern National. Eastern National provides quality educational products and services to America's national parks and other public trusts.

The 1997 edition was made possible with the generous support and assistance of the Trustees of the Saint-Gaudens Memorial.

The 2002 edition—we graciously acknowledge the generous support of the National Gallery of Art, Washington, D.C.

Printed in the United States of America.
Design: Barbara Jones

ISBN 1-888213-91-4
Eastern item number: 2-29502

Eastern National
c/o Saint-Gaudens National Historic Site
RR 3, Box 73
Cornish, NH 03745

CONTENTS

PREFACE

"It was a consecration" the sculptor Augustus Saint-Gaudens recalled on that glorious day in May 1897, when his monument was unveiled on Boston Common. That story and the history of the Fifty-Fourth Massachusetts Regiment is ever worthy of retelling. Gregory Schwarz has given us not only the complete history of the Monument; but also the heroism and events of the Fifty-Fourth Regiment of African-American troops in the Civil War; the Battle of Fort Wagner and its importance in American history. Through his study, especially from the writings of the veteran of the regiment, Capt. Luis F. Emilio's *A Brave Black Regiment,* as well as the host of other publications on the Regiment, he has provided us a full account of the great sacrifice of those who served. As General Colin Powell so movingly said in his speech to those gathered in Boston on May 31, 1997, the 100th anniversary of the monument, "they are covered in glory everlasting."

In conjunction with that celebration, the Friends of the Boston Common continue the restoration and preservation of the monument in Boston. At the same time, the Trustees of the Saint-Gaudens Memorial, a non-profit organization associated with the Saint-Gaudens National Historic Site in Cornish, New Hampshire, undertook the production of a bronze cast of the Monument directly from the original plaster which had been exhibited since 1901. Their gift to the nation of the bronze, preserves not only this final version, but also allowed the National Park Service the opportunity to place the monumental cast on long-term loan to the National Gallery of Art in Washington, D.C. It was restored and installed in a gallery where it is viewed by many thousands of visitors each year. This joint effort is retold in the essay by National Park Service conservator, Brigid Sullivan. In this new edition of the book we are fortunately able to have a foreword by Professor Vincent Scully, adapted from the fine speech that he presented in July 1997 at the dedication in Cornish.

For Augustus Saint-Gaudens, the monument was a labor of love. In our commentary we often say that the sculptor worked on it for fourteen years before it was unveiled in Boston in 1897. However as we learn here, he continued to work on the plaster cast for another three years, making this a unique and final version.

Almost immediately after its unveiling on Boston Common, the Shaw Memorial and the sculptor, Augustus Saint-Gaudens, have been a source of great inspiration. Among these are the narrative poem by Robert Lowell; the symphonic trilogy "Three Places in New England" the first of which is entitled, "The Shaw in Boston Common, Moving, Marching, Faces of Souls" by composer Charles Ives. Most recently we have experienced it through the wonderfully dramatized film documentary, *Glory.* These and other commemorations are recounted here in Larry Lauerhass' essay.

I would like to take this opportunity to thank Byron Bell, president of the Saint-Gaudens Memorial and the officers, trustees and donors who made the preservation project and the first edition of this book possible. We are most grateful to Earl Powell, director, as well as the friends and staff of the National Gallery of Art for their stewardship in the continued preservation and interpretation of the monument in Washington, D.C.

John H. Dryfhout
Superintendent
Saint-Gaudens National Historic Site, Cornish, NH

FOREWORD

Saint-Gaudens' Memorial to Colonel Shaw and the 54th Massachusetts, Boston's regiment of black infantry, may well be the greatest piece of public sculpture ever made in the United States, the one which embodies best our country's most enduring tragedy, its hope, and our common fate. It was conceived and executed in the late nineteenth century, at a time when American public architecture and sculpture were at their best and most integrated with each other, and when many veterans of the regiment were still able to parade before the images of themselves.

It was very moving to me to be invited to speak at the unveiling of the new, golden, gleaming cast of the Shaw Memorial at Cornish in 1997, but it was hard to know what to say that might be worthy of the occasion. Orators in the nineteenth century seemed able to use words like honor and duty very easily to praise other men's deaths or to induce them to die. It's harder today, hard to find words true enough to describe the devotion of Colonel Shaw and the men of the 54th, their pain, their bravery, and the transcendent achievement of Saint-Gaudens in calling them back for us as if they were alive once more.

The Memorial began as an equestrian monument to Shaw. Saint-Gaudens tells us, with touching candor, that he began work on the commission as a young sculptor interested in the horse, and only became aware of what was involved here as his long years of work went on: first the horse, then the Colonel, and then the men, at first only as a background for Shaw. Today the men are perhaps the most wholly real of all. As William James said, ". . . the bronze Negroes breathe." Last was the angel, or the victory, or what she may be, and Saint-Gaudens had endless trouble with her, probably because she was not a living being like the others. Allegorical figures did not come easily to modern artists even then.

We are reminded, though, that what Saint-Gaudens shows us here is an ancient, archetypal scene. One of the earliest works of art we have from the first cities constructed by mankind is a sculptural relief of a Sumerian king leading his infantry into battle. He is bigger than they are. Another, much later, on the Arch of Titus in Rome, has the legions parading in a dense mass with the spoils of Jerusalem, while on the columns of Trajan and Marcus Aurelius they march with their emperors in a long upward spiral to our right, in which the figures of the rulers constantly reappear.

But no sculptured soldiers anywhere move quite as these do: modeled and cast in light and shade with infinite subtlety like a painting rising up into three dimensions, all together at last in the illusion of solid depth, all one phalanx moving forward, supporting, indeed buoying up, the horse and the rider, wheeling inexorably out into the light and then into the darkness, with death and victory floating over them all.

The deed this relief records is one of blood and terror. It is a march to death in a common cause, nothing less—beyond all words—than the liberation of human beings from chattel slavery and the establishment of black men as equals and soldiers. And beyond all words Saint-Gaudens sets these people out in space as only a great sculptor can do, populating our world with their living bodies, filling it with their will to act, their resolve, marching down Beacon Street just as they in fact marched off to the war. In them, still alive, is Abolitionist Boston at its climactic hour.

We have other things in our public sculpture today, irony and menace and wit, but not this Greek confidence in the beauty of mankind, not this conviction, this Roman courage. It fills us especially here because we know how this march ended: in an unwavering frontal assault on an impregnable position. Colonel Shaw was one of the first to fall, with his orderly sergeant at his side. His body was stripped of its uniform and tipped over into the bottom of a burial ditch, and his men were thrown in on top of him.

The facts are hard. It was Shaw who chose. We know that his commanding officer, who was also mortally wounded in the assault, gave Shaw every encouragement not to commit the 54th. "Your men, I know, are worn out," he said. But Shaw would have none of that for his people. "I want you to prove yourselves," he said.

Many years ago, Allen Tate, a great Southern poet, wrote "Ode to the Confederate Dead," a fine true poem about death: no names, no acts, all graveyard and the little green snake that inherits it all. But when Robert Lowell of Boston responded to his teacher, Tate, by writing "For the Union Dead," he wrote about a regiment, the 54th Massachusetts, and he commemorated Saint-Gaudens' Memorial itself. Most of all, writing in the great days of the Civil Rights Movement, Lowell brought its meaning up to date as a precept of the kind of civic virtue, indeed of the individual's responsibility for the community, that he felt the United States most needed to hear about then. It remains timely.

Lowell still focused on Shaw but dedicated his poem to the whole regiment. For Saint-Gaudens' Latin motto on the relief, OMNIA RELINQUIT SERVARE REM PUBLICAM, which refers only to Shaw, "He gave up everything to serve the republic," Lowell substituted, Relinquunt Omnia Servare Rem Publicam: "They gave up everything. . . ." It is their monument that "sticks like a fishbone / in the city's throat." It is Shaw who "has an angry wrenlike vigilance, . . ." who ". . . cannot bend his back," and who commits them all. But it is they, as Saint-Gaudens finally realized, who carry him along.

Vincent Scully

Vincent Scully is Sterling Professor Emeritus of the History of Art, Yale University. He retired in 1991, however still teaches at Yale in the fall and is Distinguished Visiting Professor at the University of Miami in the spring.

Col. Robert Gould Shaw (1837-1863).
Courtesy U.S. Military History Institute.

THE MASSACHUSETTS FIFTY-FOURTH REGIMENT

by Gregory C. Schwarz

*The Negroes fought gallantly, and were headed
by as brave a colonel as ever lived.*
—Lt. Iradell Jones, Confederate Army

The Massachusetts Fifty-Fourth Regiment was the first military unit raised in the North of "persons of African descent." Though there were many other units of African Americans during the Civil War, this regiment was the most famous at the time and remains so today. It was the brave conduct of the Fifty-Fourth during the attack on Fort Wagner near Charleston, South Carolina, in July 1863, which helped inspire widespread enlistment of blacks into the Union forces.

Early in the war, white abolitionists joined black leaders like Frederick Douglass in calling for enlistment of African Americans into the army but there was widespread prejudice in the North against taking this step. Despite the fact that blacks served with American forces during the Revolution and in subsequent conflicts, many whites believed that African Americans would fight poorly, if at all, and were incapable of learning military discipline. Even President Lincoln was hesitant to officially approve this measure.

With the signing of the Emancipation Proclamation on January 1, 1863, Congress reluctantly authorized the raising of regiments composed of African Americans, but required that the officers be white. Governor John A. Andrew of Massachusetts was one of the first to raise such a regiment. An abolitionist himself, Andrew was an early supporter of enlisting black soldiers.

When Governor Andrew looked for a colonel to head the new regiment, he immediately thought of Robert Gould Shaw, son of George and Sarah Blake (Sturgis) Shaw, a prominent Bostonian family. The Shaws were also staunch abolitionists and strongly supported the formation of an African American regiment. After being contacted by the Governor, Shaw's father at once sent word to his son, then on duty in Virginia with the Massachusetts Second Regiment, to apprise him of Andrew's offer.

Robert Gould Shaw was born in Boston on October 10, 1837 and as a young man, studied and traveled in Europe. After his return to the United States, he enrolled at Harvard University, but withdrew in his junior year to work for his uncle, Henry P. Sturgis, who had a mercantile business in New York City. Shaw soon found that he disliked this type of work, and on April 19, 1861, answered President Lincoln's call for troops and enlisted in the Seventh New York Regiment. Shaw's unit was sent to Virginia, but he saw no action during his short time with them.

On May 28, 1861, Shaw received a commission as second lieutenant in the Massachusetts Second Regiment. By July 8, 1861, he was made a first lieutenant, and on August 10, 1862, was promoted to captain. It was during his service with the Second Massachusetts, that he saw his first combat, fighting in several small skirmishes and the battles of Cedar Mountain and Antietam, where he was wounded in the neck. In one battle he was spared a mortal wound when his gold pocket watch deflected a bullet.[1]

Shaw's first reaction upon receiving Governor Andrew's offer to command the Fifty-Fourth was to refuse. He preferred to stay with his regiment where he had friends and felt confident of rapid advancement. Shaw however knew that this new regiment was an important experiment and had reservations about being the best man for the post. He wrote a letter declining the offer, but the very next day, reconsidered and decided to accept. Shaw felt it might be cowardly of him to refuse, and he also did not want to disappoint his parents.

Recruiting poster, 1863.
Courtesy Massachusetts Historical Society.

The formation of a black regiment met with indignation in the South. Upon learning of this action, the Confederate Congress issued a proclamation stating that African Americans captured in uniform would be sold into slavery. White officers leading such regiments would be considered as inciting servile insurrection and executed. While this threat was never put into practice with captured Union troops, at the time it posed a very real and serious threat for black and white soldiers alike, and was especially troublesome to those who were once slaves.

Recruiting began in Boston on February 9, 1863, and by February 21, barracks were established at Camp Meigs in Readville, Massachusetts, just outside of Boston. It soon became apparent that enlistments from Massachusetts alone would be insufficient to quickly fill the regiment. Recruitment was therefore initiated elsewhere in New England, as well as New York, Indiana, Missouri, Ohio, and even Canada. Later, these states would form their own regiments of African American volunteers, but at this time the idea was untested, and recruiters met with widespread prejudice against enlistment of blacks. In some instances, in order to avoid trouble, new recruits were sent to Readville in small groups under cover of darkness.

Training began in earnest as soon as the first recruits arrived. Shaw, at first dubious about the abilities of the recruits, quickly found them responding well to military discipline. He even commented that they were better in this respect than the Irish troops with whom he served in other regiments.

By May 12, 1863, the regiment finally reached its full strength of 1,000 men and consisted of ten companies designated A through I, and K. The men were issued standard Union infantry uniforms of light blue. Shaw insisted that his men not be issued the darker blue uniform then designated for orderlies and African American civilians working for the army. The troops also received the .577 cal. Enfield rifled musket. Imported from England, these rifles were used in great numbers by both sides during the war.

On May 18, 1863, Governor Andrew presented the Regiment with its colors. Four flags were received; a national flag, the Massachusetts state flag, a regimental standard of white silk with the figure of the Goddess of Liberty, and the motto "Liberty, Loyalty, and Unity," and another flag with a cross upon a blue field, and the motto, *In Hoc Signo Vinces* (In this sign, victory).

Soon thereafter, a private in Company A, was inspired to write the song "Hoist the Flag," with the chorus:

> Oh! give us a flag all free without a slave,
> We'll fight to defend it as our fathers did so brave.
> The gallant Comp'ny A will make the rebels dance;
> And we'll stand by the Union, if we only have a chance.[2]

Also on May 18, a request came from General David Hunter, commanding the Department of the South, asking that Shaw's regiment proceed to Beaufort, South Carolina. Ten days later, on the morning of May 28, 1863, the regiment broke camp and made a grand march through

Boston. Colonel Shaw rode at the head of his troops. As they passed his parents' home at 44 Beacon Street, he turned to his family gathered on the balcony and raised his sword to his lips. There, along with his parents and sisters stood his wife of three weeks, Anne Kneeland Haggerty.

Also watching the troops was the famous orator and black leader, Frederick Douglass. Early in the war, Douglass spoke widely on the idea that African Americans should be allowed to enlist in the army to fight for the Union. His sons, Lewis and Charles, joined the regiment when it was formed, both would survive the war.

The reception from the populace was one of encouragement and excitement. Crowds lined the streets, but there were

Frederick Douglass (1817-1895)

no obvious incidents of disrespect. Unbeknownst to most onlookers, however, additional police were kept in reserve out of sight in case of trouble. During the march, the regiment passed in front of the State House where Governor Andrew waited with his staff, past the very spot where thirty-four years later the Memorial would stand. As the regiment continued on its way to the harbor, the band struck up the popular tune *John Brown's Body*.

Among the onlookers in Boston that morning, was the abolitionist and pacifist poet, John Greenleaf Whittier. Throughout the war he steadfastly refused to look at any troops, or write verse that in any way would contribute to armed conflict. He did, however, watch the Fifty-Fourth that day, and later wrote: "The only regiment I ever looked upon during the war was the Fifty-Fourth Massachusetts on its departure for the South. I can never forget the scene as Colonel Shaw rode at the head of his men. The very flower of grace and chivalry, he seemed to me beautiful and awful, as an angel of God come down to lead the host of freedom to victory."[3]

The regiment embarked on the new transport, *De Molay*, arriving at Hilton Head Island, South Carolina, on June 3, 1863. Here they came under the overall command of Major General David Hunter. An enthusiastic proponent of black troops, in 1862, Hunter formed the First Regiment of South Carolina Volunteers from among runaway and freed slaves. Unlike the volunteers recruited for the Fifty-Fourth, not all of Hunter's men joined willingly. Some Union officers later commented that his efforts were a good example of how not to go about enlisting African American troops. Hunter's first black regiment, formed without official orders, was quickly disavowed by the Federal government. Early the next year, however, permission was granted for Hunter to proceed with his venture and by the time the Fifty-Fourth arrived, he had reorganized this regiment. In addition to this unit, by May 1863, Hunter's subordinate, Colonel James Montgomery, had formed another black Regiment, The Second South Carolina Volunteers.

On June 10, Montgomery asked that Shaw's troops accompany his regiment on a foraging expedition inland to Darien, Georgia. Shaw was excited to have his men participate in this raid, their first action against the enemy, but soon discovered that Montgomery's primary aim appeared to be looting. Darien was a small, pleasant town of no military value, and the few enemy troops stationed there had withdrawn. After looting the town, Montgomery ordered the buildings set afire. Shaw protested the burning, but he and his men were forced to concede to direct orders. Only one company of the Fifty-Fourth actually participated in setting the fires.

Disheartened by the episode in Darien, Shaw wrote to General Strong on July 6, and asked that the Fifty-Fourth be transferred to Strong's command in a more active theater of the war. He asserted that it was important to have black troops be associated with white soldiers as much as possible so there would be other witnesses to their capabilities. The General complied with Shaw's request and two days later the regiment was transferred to James Island, South Carolina under Strong's command.

It was on James Island that the regiment received its first taste of real combat. On July 16, while manning a picket line, they were attacked by a superior number of Confederate troops intent on recapturing the island. The Fifty-Fourth stubbornly held the line in hand to hand fighting until they were able to withdraw in good order. The Regiment's stand allowed three companies of the Tenth Connecticut, stationed in a very precarious position, to escape certain destruction or capture. Their bravery, though, came at a price of eleven dead, thirteen captured and twenty-four wounded.[4]

The bombproof at Fort Wagner that protected the garrison during the artillery bombardment.
Photograph taken after occupation by Union forces. Courtesy U.S. Military History Institute.

The soldiers retired to nearby Morris Island, where strong Confederate gun batteries stood at Fort Wagner guarding Charleston harbor. Federal troops occupied most of the island with the objective of taking this fort as they felt it was essential to breaking the defense of Charleston. If Fort Wagner were captured, Fort Sumter and other defenses would then be open to fire from Union land-based batteries and could be more easily subdued.

Battery Wagner, as it was known by its defenders, was a massive earthwork fortification situated on a small peninsula at the northern end of Morris Island. The only approach for the troops was along a narrow spit of land with the ocean on one side and a marsh on the other. This fort's earthworks were said to be the largest ever made to that time during the war. Behind the walls was a "bombproof" of earth and sandbags, which served as a bunker to protect the 1,700 man garrison during artillery bombardments. Armaments included a number of large artillery pieces that could shoot both solid shot and canister. The latter consisted of a projectile filled with a mass of small iron balls, 1-2 inches in diameter. When fired it had a shotgun-like effect that could prove devastating to attacking troops.

Though a Union attack on Wagner the previous week was repulsed with heavy casualties, General Seymour, the overall Union commander, wanted to make another frontal assault believing he could still capture the fort. Most of the other officers in his command thought it would be fruitless against such strong defenses. Colonel Shaw was anxious for the chance to prove his men in combat, and when meeting with General Strong, asked him to allow the Fifty-Fourth to participate in the upcoming battle. At this point, Shaw's men had received virtually no rest and little food for the last two days, but this was the opportunity they had wanted. Strong, aware of the men's situation, replied, "your men, I know, are worn out, but do as you choose."[5] Shaw's regiment was placed in the vanguard of the attack.

A heavy artillery bombardment from Union sea and land batteries hit the fort with an enormous barrage. The shelling, however, proved ineffective against the sandbagged guns and earthworks. When the firing ceased, none of the Confederate cannon were damaged and the garrison suffered only eight killed and twenty wounded. By the time the Fifty-Fourth began their fateful charge, the entire defense armament of the fort was ready for them.

Because of sickness, the casualties suffered at James Island, and a strong guard left at their camp, only 600 men of the Fifty-Fourth were actually involved in the battle. They arrived at the assembly point about 3:00PM then marched to within 1,000 yards of Fort Wagner where they waited. Besides the Fifty-Fourth in the first wave of the assault, white troops from Connecticut, New York and New Hampshire regiments were to follow in a second wave.

At 7:45PM, when it was almost dark, Shaw gave the command to advance. One officer remembered that Shaw first encouraged the men by saying "I want you to prove yourselves. . . . The eyes of thousands will look on what you do tonight."[6] When the trooops were within a hundred yards of the fort, Shaw ordered the charge. He had instructed the men not to shoot during the advance but to use their bayonets. As the soldiers ran toward the fort they met with a withering fire from musket and cannon. Men fell wounded or dead with each enemy volley, but the regiment pressed on climbing through a ditch and up the sloping walls of the earthworks.

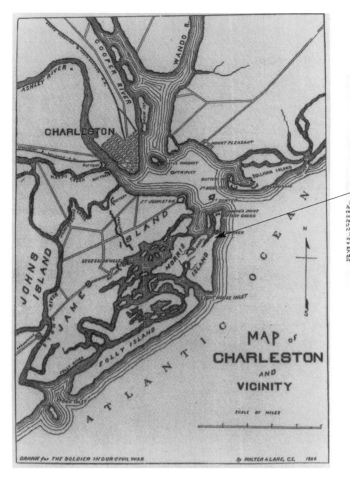

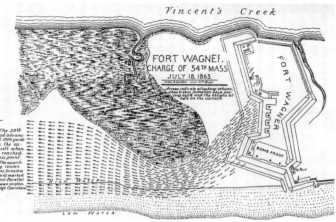

Map of the battle of Fort Wagner, July 18, 1863.
From Luis F. Emilio, *A Brave Black Regiment (1891).*

Shaw at the head of his men mounted the top of the parapet with his sword in the air and shouted "forward Fifty-Fourth."[7] At that very moment he toppled forward, shot in the chest. Others also made it to the top of the wall including the standard bearer. He too was killed, but as he fell, Sergeant William Carney grabbed the flag. Though badly wounded in the chest and arms, Carney eventually made it back to camp later that night. Still holding the tattered flag, he entered the hospital tent and remarked to his comrades "I never let the dear old flag touch the ground boys."[8] Congress later awarded Carney the Medal of Honor for his actions, the first African American so honored.

Clara Barton, the nurse who later founded the American Red Cross, watched the battle from the Union flagship, "I saw the bayonets glisten . . . and the dark line of blue trailed into the belching walls of Wagner. I saw them on, up and over the parapets into the jaws of death, and heard the clang of the death-dealing sabers as they grappled with the foe. I saw . . . the wounded, slowly crawling to me down the tide-washed

Storming Fort Wagner. Chromolithograph by Kurz & Allison (Chicago, 1890).

The splendid 54th is cut to pieces.

—Lewis H. Douglass

---

beach."[9] Praise even came from a Confederate lieutenant, Iredell Jones, "The Negroes fought gallantly, and were headed by as brave a colonel as ever lived. He mounted the breastworks waving his sword, at the head of his regiment, and he and an orderly sergeant fell dead over the inner crest of the works."[10]

Harriet Tubman, black Union scout and famed "conductor" for the "underground railway," also witnessed the battle, "And then we saw de lightning, and that was de guns; and then we heard de thunder, and that was de big guns; and then we heard de rain falling, and that was de drops of blood falling; and when we came to get in de crops, it was dead men that we

*Sgt. William H. Carney holding the flag he saved
at Fort Wagner.* Courtesy U.S. Military History Institute.

reaped."[11] Tubman later helped nurse the wounded and bury the dead.

The next morning a truce was declared while the dead were buried, although the Confederates refused an offer of Union assistance and did the work themselves. A Union prisoner, Assistant Surgeon, John T. Luck, captured during the battle, reported being shown the body of a colonel and an African American sergeant lying side by side. The other white officers that fell were given an honorable burial, but he related that Shaw, stripped of his uniform was thrown into a common grave with the enlisted men. This was intended as an insult because of Shaw's command of black troops. The surgeon claimed that the Confederate commander,

Brigadier General Hagood, remarked "I had known Shaw before the war and he was an honorable man. Had he been in command of white troops, I should have given him an honorable burial; as it is, I shall bury him in the common trench with the Negroes that fell with him."[12] After the war Hagood denied having known Shaw, or saying anything of this nature, claiming the dead were simply buried quickly because of the heat. Northern papers, however, reported the quote as the more inflammatory, "He is buried with his niggers," which aroused indignation in the North and helped the recruiting efforts for new black regiments.

After the battle, the Union commanders changed their tactics and decided to lay siege to Fort Wagner, as well as continue an unrelenting artillery bombardment. Finally, on September 6, the Confederate defenders abandoned the battered fort and it was quickly occupied by Union troops, including the Fifty-Fourth. An effort was then planned to recover Shaw's body for proper burial. When his parents heard of this, they immediately wrote to General Gilmore and requested that their son's body not be disturbed. "We hold that a soldier's most appropriate burial place is on the field where he has fallen."[13] Because of relentless erosion of the sea, much of the fort and the burial site of those slain during the battle is now under water.

Total Union casualties in the battle amounted to 1,515, while the Confederates suffered only 171. Among the Fifty-Fourth, at least nineteen men were captured and held at prisons in and around Charleston, and of these, at least ten later died. Forty-seven men were listed as missing, most probably killed during the attack. Over 149 were wounded in the battle, of whom at least twenty-five died of their wounds. In all, the regiment suffered 281 casualties among the 600 men who fought that day, a casualty rate of almost 50 percent.[14] White troops in the second wave of the assault also endured high casualties including General Strong, who was mortally wounded. Among the New Hampshire troops killed was Brigadier General Haldimand S. Putnam, a native of Cornish, NH.[15] Coincidentally, it was in this small New England town that sculptor Saint-Gaudens would later establish a studio and spend the last seven years of his life.

Shortly after the battle, Edward L. Pierce, correspondent for the *New York Daily Tribune*, spoke with the mortally wounded General Strong. Strong's remarks echoed those of many other observers: "The Fifty-fourth did well and nobly . . . They moved up as gallantly as any troops could, and with their enthusiasm they deserved a better fate."[16]

1 2

3 4

Men of the Fifty-Fourth

1. Sgt. Henry Steward (1840-1863), Courtesy Massachusetts Historical Society.

2. Henry Monroe (1845-1913), Courtesy Massachusetts Historical Society.

3. Lt. Peter Vogelsang (1815-1887), Courtesy Massachusetts Historical Society.

4. Sgt. Francis Fletcher (ca. 1841-1878) 4 x 2½ in. Courtesy U.S. Department of Interior, National Park Service, Saint-Gaudens Historic Site, Cornish, NH. Gift of Patricia and Carleton Clement, 1997.

Besides Shaw, two other officers of the Fifty-Fourth were killed in the assault and many wounded, including Lt. Col. Edward Hallowell. After his recovery, it was Hallowell who took over command of the regiment, and he remained in this position for the remainder of the war.

On February 20, 1864, the regiment joined in a campaign across northern Florida under the command of General Truman Seymour. While marching toward Tampa, they were attacked by a superior Confederate force near Olustee. The battle was a Southern victory, but the Fifty-Fourth fought a commendable rear guard action to protect the withdrawal of troops, saving many from certain capture. Again, the unit won praise for their action. During the battle, several men of the Fifty-Fourth were captured and sent to the notorious Andersonville prison. One of these, Corporal James Henry Gooding, who later died at Andersonville, wrote numerous letters home during his service for publication in the hometown newspaper, the New Bedford, Massachusetts, *Mercury*. In 1991, these were compiled into a book, *On the Altar of Freedom: A Black Soldier's Civil War Letters From the Front*.

One major issue involving the Fifty-Fourth was that of their pay scale. Though promised the standard pay of $13, the government only wanted to give soldiers in black regiments $10 a month, the wage of black laborers working for the army. In protest, Shaw and his men refused to take their pay until they received the same amount as the white troops. It was not until June 15, 1864, eleven months after the attack on Fort Wagner, that this issue was finally resolved through an act of Congress. Only then were the men authorized to receive an amount equal to that of white soldiers. Though the action was retroactive, the long delay in receiving any pay caused hardships for many of the soldiers' families.

The Fifty-Fourth fought in two other larger battles during the remainder of the war, one at Honey Hill, South Carolina on November 30, 1864, and the last on April 18, 1865, at Boykins Mills, South Carolina, nine days after Robert E. Lee surrendered at Appomattox Courthouse.

On September 1, 1865, the men of the Fifty-Fourth received their final payments and discharge papers. The following day, the regiment landed in Boston where they marched through the streets to the State House as they had over two years before, greeted once again by cheering crowds. Governor John Andrew met them at the State House, and after a ceremonial return of the flags and a farewell address by Colonel Hallowell, the regiment officially disbanded. Thirty-two years later some of the veterans would return to this spot to march together one last time to pay homage to their regiment and the memory of their commander on the unveiling of the monument.

By the end of the war, over 175,000 African American men had enlisted in the Federal army and navy, accounting for ten percent of the total armed forces. After those first battles near Charleston in July 1863, the role of the United States Colored Troops continually increased in importance and effect. By the end of the conflict, President Lincoln is said to have remarked that participation of African American men in the service was critical in winning the war for the Union.[17]

Augustus Saint-Gaudens (1848-1907). Age 33.
Courtesy U.S. Department of Interior,
National Park Service, Saint-Gaudens Historic Site, Cornish, NH.
George C. Cox, photographer, ca 1881.

THE SHAW MEMORIAL:
A HISTORY OF THE MONUMENT

by Gregory C. Schwarz

A Symphony in Bronze

The *Shaw Memorial* remains one of sculptor Augustus Saint-Gaudens' most inspiring and celebrated masterpieces and is considered by some to be America's greatest public monument. It is also the sculpture that took him the longest to complete: fourteen years from when he first began sketching his ideas with pencil and clay until the unveiling on Boston Common in 1897. Saint-Gaudens then worked another three years refining elements of the monument until it met with his total satisfaction. The sculpture's development spanned much of Saint-Gaudens' career, from the time he first achieved fame in 1881, until he reached the height of his recognition in the world of art, when awarded a gold medal at the Paris Exposition in 1900.

Augustus Saint-Gaudens was born March 1, 1848, in Dublin, Ireland, to a French shoemaker, Bernard Saint-Gaudens and his Irish wife, Mary McGuiness. Six months later, the family emigrated to New York City, where Augustus grew up. After completing school at age thirteen, he apprenticed with a cameo cutter, at the same time taking night classes at the Cooper Union and the National Academy of Design. At nineteen, his apprenticeship completed and his mind set on becoming a sculptor, he traveled to Paris where he studied at the renowned École des Beaux-Arts.

In 1870, Saint-Gaudens left Paris for Rome, where for the next five years he studied classical art and architecture and worked on his first commissions. Here, he also met an American art student, Augusta Homer of Boston, whom he later married. In 1876, he received his first major commission, a monument to Civil War Admiral David Glasgow Farragut. Unveiled in New York in 1881, the work was a tremendous success; its combination of realism and allegory was a departure from previous American sculpture. Saint-Gaudens' fame grew, and during his career he created public monuments to other Civil War heroes: the *General John A. Logan Monument*; *Lincoln, The Man*; *Lincoln, Head of State*; the *Sherman Monument* and the *Shaw Memorial*.

The origins of the *Shaw Memorial* began shortly after the battle of Fort Wagner, when men of the Fifty-Fourth proposed to erect a memorial to their fallen Colonel. Even though the issue of equal pay remained unsettled, and they had not yet received their money, the men raised $2,832. An additional $1,000 was contributed by the men of Thomas Wentworth Higginson's African American Regiment, and another $300 by the black population of Beaufort, South Carolina.[18]

The first thought was to locate a simple monument on Morris Island near Fort Wagner and the mass burial site. Shaw's father suggested at that time "The monument, though originated for my son, ought to bear, with his, the names of his brave officers and men, who fell and were buried with him. This would be but simple justice. . . ."[19] Because of local hostility, as well as unstable ground conditions, the monument was never erected. However, the funds instead went to support a worthy cause, financing Charleston's first free school for African American children, which was named in honor of Shaw.

Colonel Shaw became a martyr among northern abolitionists, and in 1864, a young sculptor, Edmonia Lewis (1845-1909), completed a portrait bust of him. Lewis' father was African American and her mother part Native American (Chippewa). Lewis sold numerous plaster casts of the sculpture, and used the proceeds to finance a trip to Europe where she studied sculpture. While there, she completed a marble copy of the Shaw bust (now in the collections of the Museum of Afro American History, Boston).

Shaw was also remembered in other ways. The New Bedford, Massachusetts post of the Grand Army of the Republic (GAR), a national organization of Union veterans, was named the Shaw Post in his honor. Most of the men in "C" Company of the Fifty-Fourth came from New Bedford, home to the largest settlement of blacks in Massachusetts, second only to Boston.

In 1865, after the end of hostilities, another effort began in Boston to erect a monument closer to home. An African American businessman, Joshua Benton Smith, initiated a new call for a memorial to Colonel Shaw. A fugitive slave, Smith worked for the Shaw family when the Colonel was a child. By the 1860s, Smith had established a successful catering business in Boston, and in 1874, served in the Massachusetts leg-

Joshua B. Smith (1813-1879)
Courtesy Massachusetts Historical Society.

islature. He, along with others, met with Governor John Andrew who readily endorsed the idea for a memorial. A committee was formed of twenty-one prominent Bostonians. With the help of abolitionist senator, Charles Sumner, and they drafted a statement of purpose, "The Monument is intended not only to mark the public gratitude to the fallen hero who at a critical moment assumed a perilous responsibility, but also to commemorate that great event wherein he was a leader by which the title of colored men as citizen soldiers was fixed beyond recall."[20]

Senator Sumner soon persuaded the committee to ask his friend, the sculptor William Wetmore Story, then in Italy, to create an equestrian statue in bas relief of Shaw. Soon after this proposal, though, both Governor Andrew and Senator Sumner died, which apparently dampened the committee's initiative. The proposal was shelved for the moment, and the committee's activities languished, nor was the project pushed by the Shaw family. Fund raising continued, however, and by 1876 through contributions and judicious investments, the initial $3,161 entrusted to the treasurer, Edward Atkinson, had grown to over $7,000. That same year, a new committee formed to raise additional money, and seven years later they reported that the balance had grown to $16,656.[21] By the fall of 1881, with funds increasing enough to move forward with the project, the committee again sought to hire a sculptor.

Augustus Saint-Gaudens (1848-1907) had vaulted onto the American art scene earlier that year with his splendid monument to Civil War Admiral David Glasgow Farragut. Unveiled in New York's Madison Square Park on Memorial Day, 1881, the sculpture instantly met with wide acclaim. Saint-Gaudens' combination of realism and allegory was a change from the neo-classical style then in vogue and the base, designed by architect Stanford White, with its Art Nouveau style bas relief elements, was unlike anything seen before in this country.

Edward Atkinson's neighbor, architect Henry Hobson Richardson, recommended Saint-Gaudens to the committee as a possible sculptor for the monument. Atkinson proposed Richardson as architectural advisor to the project, a suggestion that was soon approved. When Richardson died five years later, his role was assumed by Charles Follen McKim (1847-1909), Saint-Gaudens' friend and member of the well-known New York architectural firm of McKim, Mead and White.

After some initial correspondence, Saint-Gaudens met with the committee in 1882. As was his custom, Saint-Gaudens refused to submit a proposed model for approval unless he was the chosen artist. Because of an earlier unhappy experience competing for a commission, he now steadfastly refused to participate in any open competitions for projects. The committee acquiesced. In June 1882, Saint-Gaudens wrote to Atkinson that he would prepare a model for the committee before signing the contract, since he understood that the commission would indeed be his.[22] By mid-December he completed three preliminary clay sketches and forwarded photographs to the committee. For most of the following year, Saint-Gaudens worked on sketches and plans for the Memorial, and as the project became finalized, informed the committee that he would begin work on the monument by early December 1883.[23]

The contract was signed by the committee on February 23, 1884, and sent to Saint-Gaudens at his New York studio along with a check for $1,500. For the entire project, the sculptor would receive a total of $15,000.[24] Saint-Gaudens in return, agreed to deliver the sculpture within two years. Originally conceived as a modest bas-relief, completion of such a work within this time frame seemed reasonable.

As a young sculptor, the thirty-six-year-old Saint-Gaudens viewed this commission as his chance to do a major equestrian figure. He remarked

Architectural sketch by Henry H. Richardson, c. 1882-1883. H.H. Richardson
Architectural Drawings, MON B1, Department of Printing and Graphic Arts,
Houghton Library, Harvard College Library

H.H. Richardson Architectural Drawings, MON B2, Department of Printing and
Graphic Arts, Houghton Library, Harvard College Library

"I, like most sculptors at the beginning of their careers, felt that by hook or crook I must do an equestrian statue and that here was my opportunity."[25] His first proposal, as seen in the early pencil and clay sketches, portrayed an equestrian figure of Shaw. The Shaw family, however, demurred, noting that Shaw only achieved the rank of colonel, nor was he a famous commander. They thought an equestrian figure of him would be presumptuous as such poses should only be reserved for men of the highest rank. In response, Saint-Gaudens mused, "accordingly, in casting about for some manner of reconciling my desire (to do an equestrian) with their ideas, I fell upon a plan of associating him directly with his troops in a bas relief, and thereby reducing his importance. I made a sketch showing this scheme

Early clay sketches for the Shaw Memorial, December 1882. Archival photograph, courtesy Dartmouth College Library, Hanover, NH.

. . . and the monument as it now stands is virtually what I indicated."[26]

In March 1883, while working out his ideas for the sculpture, Saint-Gaudens wrote "I have become deeply interested in Colonel Shaw and have worked at the model with an enthusiasm I have not experienced for years."[27] One part of the monument design that Saint-Gaudens decided upon almost from the beginning was a wide curving arch at the top. In a letter from his wife, Augusta, some months later, she tells him of a grandfather clock she purchased (now exhibited at Saint-Gaudens National Historic Site): "The top is shaped precisely as you propose making the top of the Shaw bas relief."[28]

In her doctoral dissertation on Saint-Gaudens, Lois Goldreich Marcus discusses in depth the origin of the sculptor's design for the monument. She discovered that the concept of portraying Shaw on horseback with marching soldiers in the background, was probably inspired, at least in part, from a painting Saint-Gaudens saw in the Louvre, *Campagne de*

Shaw Memorial, Presentation Sketch Model, 1883.
Sketch submitted for committee approval. 15 x 16 in., U.S. Department of Interior,
National Park Service, Saint-Gaudens NHS, Cornish, NH, SAGA #25.

France 1814, by Jean-Louis Ernest Meissonier.[29] This painting depicts
Napoleon Bonaparte and his officers on horseback with rows of infantry in
the background. In a letter to his wife's niece, Eugenie Nichols, then in
Paris, Saint-Gaudens asked her to secure a photograph of the work for
him, and included a quick sketch of the painting. Although Shaw was actually on foot during the attack on Fort Wagner, normal procedure in most
armies of the day was for infantry officers to be mounted while the soldiers
walked. This was the case when the regiment marched out of Boston in
1863. By portraying Shaw in an equestrian pose Saint-Gaudens showed
historical accuracy. The pose was not intended as a statement of class or
racial superiority.

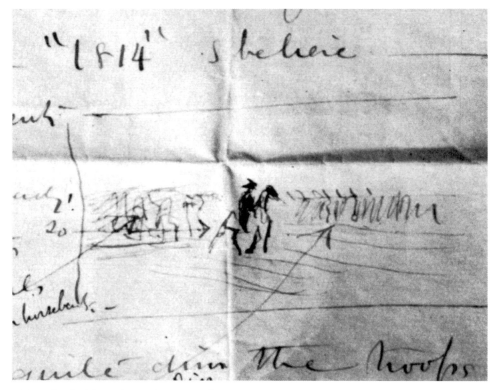

Detail of a letter from Augustus Saint-Gaudens to Eugenie Nichols, with a sketch of the Meissonier painting. Courtesy Dartmouth College Library, Hanover, NH.

Jean-Louis Ernest Meissonier, Campagne de France, 1814. Musée d'Orsay, Paris.

Early pencil sketch for the Shaw Memorial (1883).
Archival photograph, courtesy Dartmouth College Library, Hanover, NH.

Work on the *Shaw Memorial* took place entirely at Saint-Gaudens' New York studio at 148 West Thirty Sixth Street. A long, narrow structure, the building once served as a painter's supply shed. The Shaw was set against a wooden panel that stretched from wall to wall, about two thirds of the way down the room and raised about four feet from the floor. This arrangement enabled Saint-Gaudens to view the sculpture from a distance at the approximate height it would eventually be installed in Boston. In this way the perspective would be correct.

During the first few years Saint-Gaudens worked on the monument it changed considerably in concept.

> In justice to myself I must say here that from the low-relief I proposed making when I undertook the Shaw commission, a relief that reasonably could be finished for the limited sum at the command of the committee, I, through my extreme interest in it and its opportunity, increased the conception until the rider grew almost to a statue in the round and the Negroes assumed far more importance than I had originally intended. Hence the monument, developing in this way infinitely beyond what could be paid for, became a labor of love, and lessened my hesitation in setting it aside at times to make way for more lucrative commissions, commissions that would reimburse me for the pleasure and time I was devoting to this."[30]

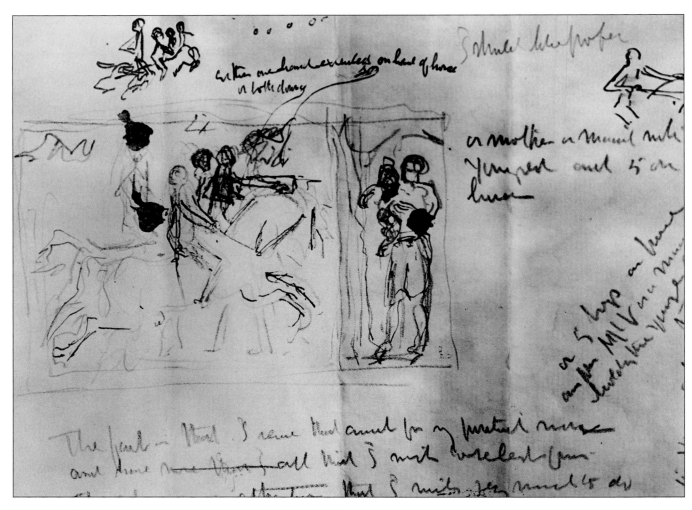

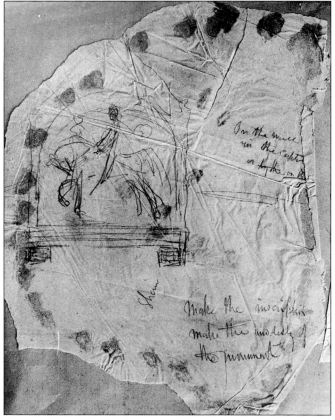

Pencil sketches for the Shaw Memorial, 1882-1883.

Courtesy Dartmouth College Library, Hanover, NH.

All Archival photograhs by Dewitt Clinton Ward, 1905.

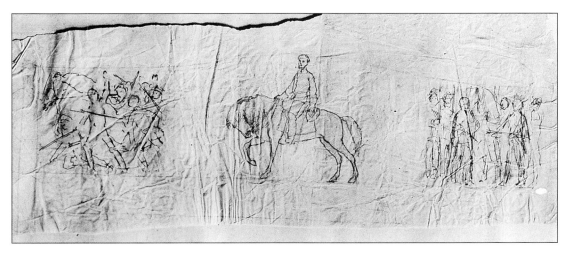

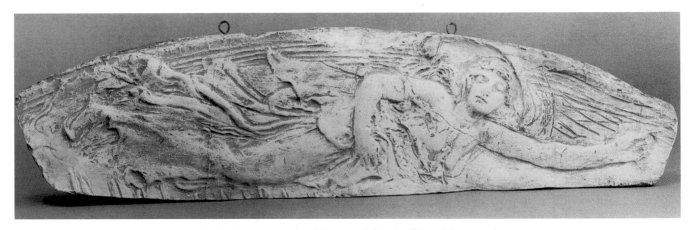

Early plaster sketch of the angel for the Shaw Memorial.
U.S. Department of the Interior, National Park Service, Saint-Gaudens NHS, Cornish, NH, SAGA #1240, 10x37 in.

First full-size clay model of the Shaw Memorial, mid 1880s.
Note head of Augustus Saint-Gaudens in lower right corner.
Archival photograph courtesy Dartmouth College Library, Hanover, NH.

Model, clay. Col. Shaw and horse, late 1880s.
This part of the monument was completed first. Archival photograph, courtesy
Dartmouth College Library, Hanover, NH.

The earliest full-scale sketch of the sculpture, though essentially the same design as the final composition, was in much lower relief than eventually used. Several other elements that were also later modified are readily noticeable. The angel faces outward, as does one soldier in the second row. The latter figure gave an almost humorous touch to the work, which was perhaps why it was not retained. The height of the drummers, at first that of grown men, was later altered to that of boys. In this first sketch the angel holds flowers, to which a palm frond signifying glory, was later added. At the last minute, in early 1897, this was changed to an olive branch signifying peace.

When working on this relief, as well as with most of his sculpture, Saint-Gaudens strove for perfection regarding realism, especially with figures. He intentionally wanted to portray a wide range of individuals, both in facial features and age, as were found among the men of the Fifty-Fourth. This was the first time a monument depicted blacks realistically, not in a stereotypical portrayal. To achieve this Saint-Gaudens hired African American men to pose. He subsequently modeled about forty different heads in one-third life size to use as studies while working on the relief. Sixteen of these likenesses are found in the final monument. In all, twenty-one recognizable faces appear among the infantrymen, along with two partial heads in very low relief. Saint-Gaudens remembered that he eliminated several of the studies which he thought quite good, simply because they did not fit well in the composition; of the six extant study heads, two match faces in the monument.

These models were not professionals, but individuals Saint-Gaudens saw on the street and who appeared to have just the look he needed for the soldiers. So particular was Saint-Gaudens on this issue, that in 1893 he wrote to his brother-in-law, Thomas J. Homer, in Boston, to ask for his assistance in hiring two men, John and Riley Lee, who worked in Young's Cafe, a Boston restaurant. He had seen them once while dining there and thought them perfect models for the monument.[31]

In his *Reminiscences,* Saint-Gaudens describes his ineffectual efforts to hire black models. Many of the men he approached suspected the sculptor of some evil intent. When several prospects entered his studio and spied brown-painted plaster heads lying around, they became alarmed and made a quick exit. Finally, someone explained to the bewildered artist that undoubtedly these men feared he was a doctor planning to murder them and use their bodies for dissection, a common rumor of the day.

Saint-Gaudens then promised to pay one black man twenty-five cents for each model he brought him. This proved a successful strategy as the next day a large group of African American men congregated in his studio and he was able to choose some that met his needs. Even so, it took several years before he found enough models that fit his requirements and could complete enough studies.

Saint-Gaudens' concern for accuracy and realism also extended to the clothing and accessories. Only twenty years after the Civil War he still had easy access to the uniforms and equipment he needed. For example, with the saddle he carefully chose the one typically used by enlisted men, which

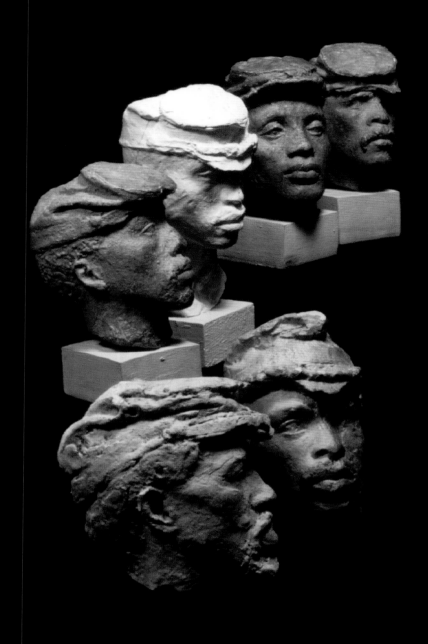

Sketch models for soldiers' heads,
U.S. Department of Interior, National Park Service, Saint-Gaudens NHS, Cornish, NH.

Sketch models for soldiers' heads.
Collections of the Saint-Gaudens
National Historic Site, Cornish, NH
Left, SAGA #1242, 5½ x 3½ x 5½ in.
Right, SAGA #1438, 5½ x 3½ x 5½ in.

Sketch models for soldiers' heads.
Collections of the Saints-Gaudens
National Historic Site, Cornish, NH
Left, SAGA #1426, 6 x 2 x 2 in.

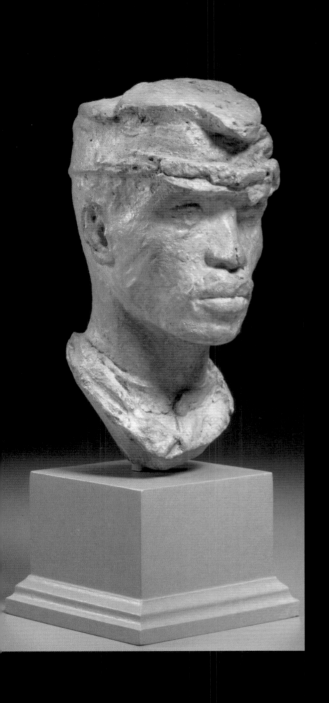

Sketch models for soldiers' heads.
Collections of the Saint-Gaudens
National Historical Site, Cornish, NH
Left, SAGA #1244, 7 x 3½ x 3 in.
Right, SAGA #1437, 5½ x 3½ x 5½ in.

Shaw Memorial, Presentation Sketch Model, 1883.
U.S. Department of Interior, National Park Service, Saint-Gaudens NHS, Cornish, NH.
SAGA #25, 15 x 16 in.

Two rows of soldiers hidden behind the horse and rider and not seen by the viewer.
Photographs taken during conservation of Shaw Memorial plaster cast, 1996.

was the type Shaw himself used and generally favored by lower ranking officers. This differed from the saddle used in the Logan and Sherman monuments which he also worked on during the 1890s.[32] To further ensure accuracy Saint-Gaudens even sent someone to sketch the original flag of the Fifty-Fourth Regiment at the State House in Boston.

Modeling some of the equipment proved troublesome as he developed the composition, especially the canteens, which he felt produced a "spotty" effect. One day, while Frederick MacMonnies, one of his sculptural assistants, worked on the canteens, Saint-Gaudens complained that he hated the way they looked in the relief. MacMonnies suggested partially covering some of them under the uniforms. Satisfied with the result, Saint-Gaudens quickly adopted the idea. From this episode he developed a system which he termed "fluing," whereby rounding off mechanically straight lines, the uninteresting became slightly hidden and suggestive. He used various ways to break up such lines and fill in deeper holes in folds of drapery, which would appear very dark and might detract from the overall effect of the sculpture.[33]

Other parts of the relief troubled the artist as well, some seemingly unimportant. Saint-Gaudens once confided to sculptor, James Earle Fraser, that there was one particular spot in the monument that he felt sure he had spent more time on than any other section. This was one of the soldier's pant legs—"it simply would not suit him and he was dragged by the impulse toward that particular fold from any other part of the monument that he might be working on." He told Fraser, "You know how you callous your hands from using the same tool for a long time. Well, I have a callous on my brain when it comes to that pant leg."[34]

The folds in Shaw's right sleeve and coat were another problem area. He could never seem to get the coat to fall quite the same way during any successive modeling session. Finally, one day in exasperation, he had one of his assistants, Lyndon Smith, pose for him in the saddle. Smith sat there from 9:00AM straight through until 4:00PM without a movement on his right side, before the modeling of Shaw's clothing was finally done to satisfaction.[35] Even this, though, he changed once again just before the monument was cast in bronze.

When he first began working on the *Shaw Memorial* Saint-Gaudens used the water-based clay commonly employed by sculptors. This type of clay had a drawback in that it had to be kept damp at all times, usually by covering the sculpture with wet rags, otherwise it would dry and crack. Keeping a work of this size moist was bothersome and time consuming. Evidence of cracks are readily visible in the photograph of the first full scale model of the relief. It was probably at about this time that Saint-Gaudens realized that the project would take much longer than he first anticipated, and began to look for an alternative to water-based clay.

The answer to the problem, he knew, was plastoline, an oil-based clay. Plastoline, still used today by sculptors, did not dry out with exposure to air. At that time it was only produced in France, and the amount needed for a project of this size was prohibitively expensive to import. As an alternative, Saint-Gaudens and a sculptural assistant, Philip Martiny, developed their own formula for plastoline. This allowed Saint-Gaudens to have the model of the Shaw Memorial stand uncovered in his studio for as long as he needed. Once he perfected the oil clay formula, Saint-Gaudens removed the full-scale sketch done in water-based clay and reconstructed it in plastoline.

Before the full sketch was redone in plastocine clay, Saint-Gaudens used the same platform to work with just the equestrian part of the memorial. The horse used for a model stood on another special platform built about four feet off the ground, the proposed height of the monument. Sometimes when the horse posed, it was not just hitched by the bridle, but tied in several places to keep it in place. When this happened, the animal protested by constantly stamping its feet and making a continual racket. The horse with the figure of Shaw became the first section finished in final form, after which it was immediately cast in plaster. Later the plaster cast of horse and rider, essentially a sculpture in the round, was placed in front of the emerging relief to see the effect, and then removed and put to the side as work progressed on the soldiers and background.

The horse Saint-Gaudens first used as a model was owned by him, "a gray animal which I bought especially for this relief. I used to keep him in an adjoining stable and, at the end of the day, ride him in the park for exercise, thereby accomplishing a double purpose. He died ultimately of pneumonia contracted from a cast I made of him, and I finished my work with a beautiful sorrel I hired at the New York Riding Club."[36] Often, to save time and effort, Saint-Gaudens and other sculptors would make a plaster cast of something they were using in a sculpture, such as articles of clothing, equipment, or even parts of animals and the human body.

Although the monument was supposed to be completed within two years, the artist ignored the deadline and proceeded at his own pace. As the years progressed, the committee understandably grew increasingly impatient. In January 1891, Saint-Gaudens wrote to Atkinson that he was working hard on the Shaw and barring illness would have the modeling done in nine months and the bronze cast three months after that.[37] By February 1893, he again wrote to Atkinson to assure him that he worked on another current commission, the World's Columbian Exposition medal, only at night, "time taken from my family and social life," and that this would in no way interfere with completion of the Shaw.[38]

While work on the relief proceeded at a slow pace, plans for the architectural setting progressed more rapidly. Charles Follen McKim designed the setting and surround for the Memorial, and on February 4, 1892, the Boston Art Commission approved his plan. Norcross Brothers Contractors of Boston and Worcester, then constructed the terrace, granite base, and Tennessee marble surround. All was completed by August 25, 1893, at a cost of $19,920 to the city of Boston.[39]

Saint-Gaudens now admitted that the monument would not be completed by the fall of 1893, but promised it by the following May. By October 1893, however, with the relief still incomplete, several committee members proposed giving the commission to Daniel Chester French, so that "the statue might be ready in the probable lifetime of some members of the committee."[40] Another letter from Atkinson to Charles McKim in 1894, stated in no uncertain terms, ". . . that bronze is wanted pretty damned quick! People are grumbling for it, the city howling for it, and most of the committee have become toothless waiting for it!"[41] This, and similar comments from others, spurred Saint-Gaudens to increase his efforts on the sculpture, but it would still be three more years until the unveiling.

In answer to criticism of why he took so long with the *Shaw Memorial*, Saint-Gaudens wrote:

> My own delay I excuse on the ground that a sculptor's work endures for so long that it is next to a crime for him to neglect to do everything that lies in his power to execute a result that will not be a disgrace. There is something extraordinarily irritating, when it is not ludicrous, in a bad statue. It is plastered up before the world to stick and stick for centuries, while man and nations pass away. A poor picture goes into the garret, books are forgotten, but the bronze remains to accuse or shame the populace and perpetuate one of our various idiocies. It is an impertinence and an offense, and that it does not create riots proves the wonderful patience of the human animal.[42]

About this time a discussion ensued among the committee, the sculptor and the Shaw family, over the inscriptions to be placed on the front and back of the monument. In June 1894, the committee approved the inscription suggested by Harvard President Charles W. Eliot: "The White Officers: The Black Rank and File: Together." Homer Saint-Gaudens related that his father's reaction was that the inscriptions for the back of the monument were to be arranged in a manner "most distasteful to him, so he began devious tactics to elude the necessity of placing them in permanent form."[43] Even at the end of February 1897, Saint-Gaudens replied to Atkinson that to place prose lines from Governor Andrew's address on the back of the monument above the officers' names "would be too much inscription on the stone" and "is out of the question to arrange it in this manner."[44]

In the background of the bronze itself, Shaw's father suggested using the motto of the Society of the Cincinnati. This was an organization formed after the Revolutionary War for officers and their descendants, and of whom Robert Gould Shaw was a hereditary member. The inscription, OMNIA RELINQVIT SERVARE REMPVBLICAM (He forsook all to preserve the public weal), was indeed used, even though the Latin is actually grammatically incorrect. In December 1898, the City of Boston Art Commission wrote to Saint-Gaudens in Paris, to say that several scholars had informed them of errors in the Latin. Perhaps feeling somewhat embarrassed, the committee wanted to correct the inscription and suggested that the artist cast a piece with the word "adpetens" and insert it after relinquit, (eagerly desiring). This, they felt, would be the easiest and most cost effective way to make the correction.[45] Their suggestion, however, was never carried out and the text remains in its original form. No doubt Saint-Gaudens felt more comfortable leaving it unchanged. Among the other symbolic details on the relief are thirty-four stars along the upper edge representing the states of the Union in 1863.

The angel, however, caused Saint-Gaudens the most problems in the composition. His sister-in-law, Elizabeth Nichols, wrote from Cornish in August 1895, "he has been working on the allegorical figure of the 'Shaw' and apparently finds it difficult to make it suit his idea. He was getting rather discouraged so he is coming here to stay until the middle of September hoping I suppose to go back refreshed."[46] For the angel's face he first used the head of Annie Page, one of his models. He soon admitted that this became too much like a portrait for him, so in the end relied on his imagination for the angel's features. Several of his long-time friends later suggested that the angel somewhat resembled his mother and also a former model in Paris. At the end of December, Saint-Gaudens wrote to Atkinson that the "floating figure" is almost done and "I'm joyous about it. I have got it at last. 'I have got it solid' as they say. I at last have what I want in it. It's a matter of cleaning it up and pulling it together now and very shortly I shall write to you 'finis'."[47]

On May 8, 1896, Saint-Gaudens reported that he finished the Shaw but that a constructional difficulty will delay its being molded for a few more weeks. He assures Atkinson it has nothing to do with the artistic portion, "that is complete." He added that the delay had created an inconvenience for him financially and requested the sum due him on finishing of the clay and would be happy with $500 or $1,000.[48]

Soon after reporting the Shaw complete, Saint-Gaudens decided to slightly alter the size of the ever-troubling angel. This prompted a quick and angry response from Atkinson on June 5, "We are all appalled and disheartened . . . by learning . . . that you have again decided to reconstruct that angel. . . . Members of the committee are hopeless of your ever being able to complete this work."[49] The next day in another letter, he told the artist "You and I are now at the parting of the ways," suggesting that "one person in a hundred thousand would ever know the difference in the angel's size."[50] Saint-Gaudens acquiesed and two days later responded by telegram that he would proceed with the monument the way it was without additional changes to the angel.[51]

On October 10, William A. Coffin, who was preparing an article on the sculptor and the *Shaw Memorial*, interviewed Saint-Gaudens. In his article, Coffin remarked that the finishing touches were put on the monument the very day he visited, which by coincidence was Colonel Shaw's birthday. The angel, as completed at this time, faced outward as in the early sketches. In her left arm she holds a palm frond, signifying victory or glory, as well as poppies denoting death. The lower half of the body and its drapery is positioned well above the level of the soldiers and their rifles. This first completed version of the *Shaw Memorial* is known only from photographs taken in preparation for Coffin's extensive article in the June 1897, issue of *Century Magazine*.[52]

Just as the monument was declared complete, and Saint-Gaudens finally satisfied with his work, he received a letter from the French sculptor, Paul Bion. As a long-time friend, Saint-Gaudens particularly valued Bion's artistic criticism. After seeing photographs of the earliest version of the Shaw, Bion responded "I had no need of your 'nom de Dieu' allegory on the ceiling. Your Negroes marching in step and your Colonel leading them told me enough. Your priestess merely bores me as she tries to impress upon me the beauty of their action."[53]

Though he had assured the committee that the sculpture was finished, Saint-Gaudens was at heart still ambivalent about the angel. Bion's comments had a profound impression on him, and he once again turned his attentions to the floating figure, making significant changes. He replaced the palm frond with an olive branch, signifying peace, redirected the angel's face forward, adding to the motion of the piece, and modified the angel's robes.[54] He even reviewed other areas of the sculpture and used the opportunity to simplify the folds in Shaw's coat where it covered the saddle. In a letter to his niece, Rose Nichols, rejoining or rebutting Bion's comments, "I am not disturbed by his dislike of my figure. It is because it does not look well in the photograph. If the figure in itself looked well, he would have liked it I know. . . . I still think that a figure, if well done in that relation to the rest of the scheme, is a fine thing to do. The Greeks and Romans did it finely in their sculpture. After all it's the way the thing's done that makes it right or wrong, that's about the only creed I have in art."[55]

Unknown to Saint-Gaudens, Bion was dead by the time he had received his letter. Later, on February 17, 1897, after hearing the sad news, he wrote to Rose Nichols,

> Today, however, I have had a kind of sad feeling of companionship with him that seems to bring him to me, in working over the head of the flying figure of the "Shaw." The bronze founders are not ready for it yet. I have had a stamp made of the figure, and I am sure you will think I have helped it a great deal. You know that Thayer [Abbot Thayer] told me he thought an idea I once had of turning the head more in profile, was a better one than that I had evolved, and I've always wished to do it. It is done, and it's the feeling of death and mystery and love, in the making of it, that brought my friend back to me so much to-day.[56]

Saint-Gaudens now worked feverishly on the relief, "I shall be all the week at the figure. I've made an olive-branch instead of the palm,—it looks less 'Christian martyr-like' and I have lightened and simplified the drapery a great deal. I had not seen it for two or three months and I had a fresh impression."[57] Homer notes that his father worked on the figure to such an extent "he became mentally blind to the result and to the aspect of the composition." Even when workmen came to pick up the cast for shipment to the foundry in December 1897, Saint-Gaudens made them wait while he made last minute changes.[58]

During the winter, while other parts of the relief were being cast, he continued to work on the angel, and by late February, sent the modified figure to the foundry for casting in place of the original version. Because Saint-Gaudens felt rushed to complete the work, he was never fully satisfied with the angel nor the way the monument appeared in Boston, and it would continue to haunt him for the remainder of his life.

James Earle Fraser recalled that Saint-Gaudens was especially delighted with criticisms of the Shaw provided by two other friends. He once asked Kenyon Cox what he thought about the piece. Cox replied that it was good, and was going along alright, adding that he was sure it would come out well in the end. Saint-Gaudens was somewhat irritated by the response and said "You are not very enthusiastic about it, are you Cox?" to which Cox replied "I am not really enthusiastic by nature—I am quiet and reserved." Just then, Saint-Gaudens' dog, Doodles, came into the studio and Cox immediately began joyfully playing with the dog exclaiming "what a grand and wonderful dog!" At which point Saint-Gaudens said "Oh, no, Cox you are not enthusiastic, you are very reserved."[59]

Another friend, painter George DeForest Brush, however, appeared somewhat upset by the monument. When Saint-Gaudens questioned him about this, he replied "Do you really want to know?" Saint-Gaudens said "Certainly, I want to know." "Well, then" said Brush, "Take out the horse!"[60]

Joy at the completion of the monument was deeply felt. McKim wrote Saint-Gaudens on September 3, 1896, "Heaven be praised! . . . I can hardly believe my eyes and am overjoyed to hear that the Shaw is really done-on your account and that of the surviving members of the committee . . ."[61]

The bronze cast was completed in May 1897, at the Gorham Manufacturing Company's foundry in Providence, Rhode Island, at a cost of $7,000. This was possibly a reduced fee, as the committee was hoping that the company would produce the complicated cast "for glory not profit." Atkinson wrote to them that he knew "it will be a difficult casting and very likely you may not make anything on it . . . yet it is a great work and well worth doing."[62]

The Monument was installed in Boston on Friday, May 21, just a week before the unveiling. The patination was only applied that weekend once the bronze was in place. Saint-Gaudens came to Boston with his assistant, Gaeton Ardisson, to oversee the process. Quick repairs were also necessary to the stonework, which though completed in 1893, stood empty and exposed to the weather for three years. During this week the monument was screened from prying eyes by a large cloth strung between the two large English elm trees that framed the site and are still there today.

Veterans of the Fifty-Fourth Massachusetts Regiment march past the Shaw Memorial at the unveiling. May 31, 1897.
Boston Sunday Journal, June 6, 1897.

THE UNVEILING

Many of them were bent and crippled, many with white heads, some with bouquets. . . . The impression of those old soldiers, passing the very spot where they left for the war so many years before, thrills me even as I write these words. They faced and saluted the relief, with the music playing "John Brown's Body," a recall of what I had heard and seen thirty years before from my cameo-cutter's window. They seemed as if returning from the war, the troops of bronze marching in the opposite direction, the direction in which they had left for the front, and the young men there represented now showing these veterans the vigor and hope of youth. It was a consecration.[65]

—Augustus Saint-Gaudens, May 31, 1897

Veteran officers of the Fifty-Fourth in front of the monument, May 31, 1897.
Courtesy Commonwealth of Massachusetts, Massachusetts Art Commission.

On May 31, 1897, the day of the unveiling, the weather was gray and overcast with a light misty rain. Saint-Gaudens, rather than complaining, commented that this type of lighting was better for viewing the monument than bright sunshine. In spite of the weather there was a festive air about the occasion, and the streets were lined with spectators. Fortunately, the rain stopped by the beginning of the ceremony. The parade began at 10:00AM as Governor John A. Andrews and various dignitaries took their place in carriages at the corner of Dartmouth and Commonwealth. Present in the reviewing party were Saint-Gaudens, Booker T. Washington, Mayor Josiah Quincy, Prof. William James, various military officers, and members of the Memorial Committee.

After the parade passed the reviewing location, the carriages conveyed the dignitaries to the site of the monument, where the men took their

*Back of the Shaw Memorial showing the inscriptions. Architectural design by Charles F. McKim.
The American Architect and Building News, September 11, 1897.*

places across the street on the State House steps. Onlookers occupied
every available space along the street and on the grounds of the State
House. People also filled the windows and balconies of the State House,
with a few of the more adventurous on the roof.

Two large American flags covered the Memorial. At exactly 11:17AM, at a
signal given by committee chairman, Colonel Henry Lee, two young
nephews of Robert Gould Shaw, stationed at the monument, pulled the
ropes that dropped the flags. As the sculpture was revealed, the crowd
cheered, the Germania Band began to play "The Battle Hymn of the
Republic" and a battery of artillery on the Common fired a seventeen-
gun salute. Simultaneously a signalman positioned on the State House
roof, waved a white flag to alert other signalmen on the Ames building.
There a large flag was dropped, to signal three Naval warships in the harbor, the U.S.S. Massachusetts, the New York and the Texas, which then
each fired a twenty-one gun salute.[63]

A brief ceremony then took place where Colonel Henry Lee, on behalf of the committee, presented the Memorial to Governor Roger Wolcott, who accepted on behalf of the Commonwealth. Lee spoke, "Friends, more than twenty years ago these subscribers appointed a committee with full powers to procure a fitting testimonial to Colonel Robert Gould Shaw and his brave black soldiers. That committee has completed its task. Your honor has witnessed the unveiling of the monument and will, I am sure, congratulate us that, thanks to the sculptor, we have builded better than we knew."[64]

The dozen or more military units present then began to march again, now past the Memorial. Included were contingents of cadets, naval seamen from the warships, and 900 members of the New York Seventh Regiment, the unit Shaw first joined during the war. Sixty-five veterans of the Massachusetts Fifty-Fourth Regiment led the parade. Some of their officers wore their Civil War uniforms, but most of the enlisted men were in their best frock coats. Black veterans from the Fifty-Fifth Massachusetts and the Fifth Cavalry were also present. Among the men of the Fifty-Fourth was Sergeant Carney carrying the American Flag. The sight of him and the flag elicited cheers from many of the onlookers who knew of his exploits. The veterans of the Fifty-Fourth returned later and laid a large wreath of Lilies of the Valley before the monument. All of this deeply moved Saint-Gaudens.

Following the parade and a special lunch for the veterans of the three African American Regiments, the festivities continued in the Music Hall. An enthusiastic audience packed the building when the ceremonies began at 12:30PM and the chorus sang *Our Heroes* and *Battle Hymn of the Republic.* Saint-Gaudens always felt extremely uncomfortable with such public occasions, and purposely arrived late so as to avoid having to sit on the podium. He was recognized, however, and quickly brought to the forefront with even more acclaim than if he had arrived early. When introduced by the Governor, Saint-Gaudens received a thunderous, standing ovation. He remembered "it was an awful moment, but it would be stupid to deny that at the same time it was thrilling to hear the great storm of applause and cheering that I faced."[66] He made sure to comment to the press that the architect Charles F. McKim deserved a great deal of credit and his contributions should not be forgotten.

Other speakers that afternoon included Prof. William James, whose brother, Garth Wilkinson James, an officer with the Fifty-Fourth, had

Portrait relief of Charles F. McKim by Augustus Saint-Gaudens., 1878.
Bronze, 7½ x 5 in
U.S. Department of Interior,
National Park Service,
Saint-Gaudens NHS, Cornish, NH,
SAGA #872.

been severely wounded at Fort Wagner. He said of the monument, "And this, fellow-citizens, is why after the great generals have had their monuments, and long after the abstract common soldiers' monuments have been reared on every village green, we have chosen to take Shaw and Shaw's regiment as the subjects of the first soldiers' monument to be raised to a particular set of comparatively undistinguished men."[67]

The other featured speaker was Booker T. Washington, president of Tuskegee Institute, and one of the most celebrated African Americans of his day. He too gave a stirring and eloquent oration that was very well received. Also on the podium to receive the acclamation of the crowd was Sergeant Carney.

Soon after the dedication, Colonel Henry Lee edited the complete proceedings of the ceremony in a finely bound, hundred-page book, *The Monument to Robert Gould Shaw*, published by the Houghton Mifflin Riverside Press in Boston. Included are the full texts of speeches, the inscriptions on the monument, and the official guest list.

Accolades on the memorial came from throughout the country and beyond. Henry James, then in Europe, saw a reproduction of the Shaw in *Harper's Weekly*, "How I rejoice that something really fine is to stand there forever for R.G.S. and all the rest of them. This thing of Saint-Gaudens strikes me as real perfection."[68] Artist and critic, Kenyon Cox, commented that "people say it's the best thing that Saint-Gaudens ever did. For my part no one anywhere in any country has ever done any better."[69]

Shaw's widow, Anne Haggerty Shaw, now an invalid and living in Cannes, France, did not attend the unveiling, but saw photos of the monument, and sent a short note congratulating the sculptor.[70] Colonel Shaw's parents were still living, and from them he received some of his most heartfelt congratulations. During his speech at the unveiling ceremony, Colonel Henry Lee quoted Shaw's mother as saying to Saint-Gaudens that day, "You have immortalized my native city; you have immortalized my dear son; you have immortalized yourself."[71] Shortly after the unveiling, Shaw's mother also asked Saint-Gaudens to visit her, which he soon did. She explained then that originally only a bas-relief had been planned, and she knew that he had spent much extra time and money on the project. In thanks, she wished to add her personal check to the amount he was paid.

The editor, Richard Watson Gilder, composed a poem on the monument, *Robert Gould Shaw*, which affected Saint-Gaudens deeply. He wrote to Gilder "that anything I have done should have suggested the inspired and inspiring ode . . . makes all the great strain and love gone to the making of the 'Shaw' worthwhile, and I have not lived entirely in vain."[72]

Sculpture court in the Grand Palais, Exposition Universelle, Paris, 1900.
The Shaw Memorial is to the left at the top of the stairway. (Report of the Commissioner-General for the United
States to the International Universal Exposition, Paris, 1900, Volume I)

PARIS

Following the unveiling of the *Shaw Memorial* in May, and the dedication in July of his monument to General John Logan, in Chicago's Grant Park, Saint-Gaudens began preparing for a move to Paris in October. He had tired of New York, and felt a desire to return to Europe. While his work was praised in America, he felt that he now needed to measure himself and his art against his contemporaries in Europe where he was less well known.

Between 1896 and 1897, he prepared a complete plaster cast of the *Shaw Memorial*, no doubt with the intention of taking it to France. In December 1897, he arranged for shipment of this cast from his New York studio along with other plaster casts, including the *Puritan*, *Amor Caritas* and the *Sherman Monument*.[73]

The Shaw Memorial at the Exposition Universelle, 1900.
(Report of the Commissioner-General for the United States to
the International Universal Exposition, Paris, 1900, Volume I)

The Shaw arrived in Paris by February 1898, and Saint-Gaudens assembled it in the studio he established in the Rue de Bagneux. Here he worked on the various changes he had contemplated since the unveiling in Boston, and in April, exhibited a reworked *Shaw Memorial* at the 1898 Paris Salon. In this third version, two noticeable changes are evident, reflecting the sculptor's unending quest for perfection. First, he lowered the angel slightly in the background, and simplified the drapery. Second, the horse's mane, which had lain down across the neck, was redesigned to flow towards the rear to further emphasize the forward motion.

For the next two years the cast remained in the Paris studio where Saint-Gaudens continued to work on it, along with other sculptures including the *Amor Caritas* and the *Sherman Monument*. In April 1900, he once again exhibited the *Shaw Memorial* in Paris, at the great *Exposition Uni-*

verselle, one of the largest expositions of its time. It was only then, seventeen years from the time he first began work on the sculpture that Saint-Gaudens finally considered the *Shaw Memorial* finished.

During the exposition, the relief stood at the top of a staircase in the Grand Palais, just outside the doorway to the United States exhibit area. Positioned to the other side of this doorway was the *Amor Caritas* or "Angel With Tablet," which the French Government later purchased for the Luxembourg Museum collection. The great central area on the ground floor was filled with sculpture, including a full sized plaster cast of the *Sherman Monument*. The Sherman would be unveiled three years later in New York's Grand Army Plaza.

Saint-Gaudens exhibited four major works in the 1900 exposition: the *Shaw Memorial*, the *Sherman Monument*, the *Puritan* and the *Amor Caritas*. He received the Grand Prix and a gold medal for his works, and was later also awarded the Legion of Honor (officier), a coveted award infrequently given to foreigners. He also received praise from the French sculptor, Auguste Rodin. When Rodin saw the *Shaw Memorial* at the Exposition, he doffed his hat in tribute to what he considered a great masterpiece.

The *Shaw Memorial* appeared now in its fourth and final form. Since its exhibition two years before, Saint-Gaudens had further modified the angel; straightening the right knee somewhat, and lowering the whole figure so that the drapery now extended down to top of the rifles. He also moved the two flags closer together and changed the position of the sword so that the blade was parallel to the relief. Along the base he added the lettering "ROBERT GOULD SHAW KILLED WHILE LEADING THE ASSAULT ON FORT WAGNER JULY TWENTY THIRD EIGHTEEN HUNDRED SIXTY THREE AUGUSTUS SAINT-GAUDENS MDCC-CLXXXXVII." (Although the inscription on the rear side of the Boston monument gives the correct date of the battle, July 18, 1863, Saint-Gaudens mistakenly used July 23 in this wording and never had it corrected).[74]

Even after initial installation at the Paris Exposition, with his sculptural changes completed, Saint-Gaudens now found himself dissatisfied with the color of the Shaw. The painter, William A. Coffin, wrote of seeing him just before the exposition opened:

> He stood at the top of the great staircase leading from the sculpture court in the Grand Palais, directing two men who were coloring the big cast of the Shaw which stood there at the entrance to the galleries occupied by the United States section in paintings. The Shaw had been colored. It was all set up and it was all

"finished." But Saint-Gaudens told me he thought it was too dark and he was having it all gone over with tint and rub-down to make it lighter. As usual he was pursuing perfection.[75]

Saint-Gaudens always showed particular concern with the patination and resulting color of a sculpture's surface. Throughout his career he utilized many different colors of patina on both bronze and plaster casts used for exhibition. He especially disliked leaving plaster casts white, because after being exhibited for a length of time they became dusty and rather dingy looking. With the Shaw, he modified the color of the plaster cast several times (1898, 1900, 1905). Once, when asked about producing additional plaster casts of the *Shaw Memorial*, he explained "I have a horror of the exhibition of my work in plaster, particularly, if it is to be permanent and unless the Shaw is colored, as is the replica at Buffalo, I could not consent to its reproduction."[76]

Paris was a great success for him artistically and marked the pinnacle of his career. Personally, however, he was dealt a heavy blow when shortly after the exposition, a French doctor diagnosed his recurring pain as colon cancer. Saint-Gaudens returned to the United States and had the cancerous tumor removed. He subsequently moved his studio to Cornish, New Hampshire permanently and equipped the place for year-round operation. In spite of declining strength, he continued to produce sculpture and survived for another seven years until his death in 1907.

BUFFALO

In 1900, William Alexander Coffin, a painter, writer and art critic, was appointed the Fine Arts Director of the Pan American Exposition planned the following year for Buffalo, New York. While in Paris visiting the Exposition Universelle, he persuaded Saint-Gaudens to exhibit some of his best work at the Exposition in Buffalo, in particular, those pieces shown in Paris. Coffin was especially familiar with the *Shaw Memorial*, having written an extensive article on Saint-Gaudens in 1897 for *Century Magazine*. He considered it a great coup to have acquired both the Shaw and Sherman for display at the exposition.

The requested casts, including the *Shaw Memorial*, the *Sherman Monument*, the *Puritan*, and the *Amor Caritas*, arrived in Buffalo by April 1901. Installed in the Fine Arts Building, the *Shaw Memorial* occupied a prominent location at the end of the Sculpture Court. Saint-Gaudens

Formal opening day of the Fine Arts Building, Pan American Exposition, Buffalo, NY, June 15, 1901.
Final touches are still being made on the Monument. The building was opened to the public two days later.
Courtesy Dartmouth College Library, Hanover, NH.

The Sculpture Court, Fine Arts Building, Pan American Exposition, Buffalo, NY. June 1901.
(Frontispiece, Catalog of the Exhibition of Fine Arts, Pan American Exposition, 1901)

Bronze cast of the angel from the fourth and final version of the Shaw Memorial, 35 13/16 in. x 9 ft. 8 1/16 in.;
made from molds taken in Buffalo 1904/5. Acquired by the Brooklyn Museum from Mrs. Augustus Saint-Gaudens, 1923.
Courtesy Brooklyn Museum, Robert B. Woodward Memorial Fund.

sent one of his young sculptural assistants, Henry Hering, to Buffalo to help assemble the large relief, make necessary repairs, and match the bronze color along the reconstructed seams. Like other very large, non-permanent sculptures, it was constructed in sections for ease in moving and casting.

The Pan American Exposition opened on May 1, 1901, but the hurriedly erected Fine Arts Building remained unfinished. Hanging of the art exhibits did not begin until May 22, two days after Dedication Day. Formal opening ceremonies for the Fine Arts Building finally took place on June 15, and it opened to the general public two days later. In a photograph taken at the opening day ceremony, one can see the Shaw cast assembled and in the process of being retouched. The relief is roped off, and a workman, possibly Hering, stands in front.

At the close of the Exposition, Coffin persisted in trying to persuade Saint-Gaudens to leave the Sherman and Shaw casts in Buffalo. As the Sherman was not yet complete, Saint-Gaudens insisted upon its return to Cornish. The Shaw, too, he wanted returned, unless he were reimbursed in the amount of $2,000. He explained that several museums, including the Art Institute of Chicago and the Dresden Museum, were interested in casts of the Shaw, and it would cost him that much to prepare a new cast from the mold he had in Cornish. After some negotiations, the Albright Knox Art Gallery purchased the piece for the requested $2,000. In the end, no additional casts of the Shaw were ever produced, possibly because of the sculptor's illness and his work on more pressing commissions. The intent to do so was there, however, as Saint-Gaudens specifically asked

Shaw Memorial on display at the Inaugural Exhibition, Albright Knox Art Gallery, Buffalo, NY, 1905.

Gaeton Ardisson, his long-time plaster casting assistant, still attending to the sculptor's affairs in Paris, to come to Cornish with the intention of making such casts.[77]

Until 1902, Saint-Gaudens exhibited the original plaster cast of the Boston version of the Shaw in the "Large Studio" in Cornish. In a letter to William Coffin in December 1901, he refers to it as a cast of the "imperfect original."[78] Sometime before 1905 he had it destroyed and buried on the grounds nearby.[79] The original mold of the Boston version was also returned from the Gorham foundry, but this too he destroyed soon after his return from Paris. Saint-Gaudens wanted to ensure that no other cast of this second version of the Shaw, which he considered flawed, could be easily produced. Any additional casts to be made he planned to do from the final version exhibited in Paris and Buffalo.

The *Shaw Memorial* plaster cast in Buffalo was moved to the new Albright Art Gallery building and set up in mid December 1901. The Albright building was originally intended to serve as the Fine Arts building for the Pan American Exposition. Because of a shortage of material, this building remained incomplete until 1905. Prior to the opening of the Albright's inaugural exhibition, the museum decided to relocate the relief to another spot within the building. This last minute decision to move the piece was made in the midst of applying a new surface treatment of gold leaf with a bronze tone glaze. This was being done by one of Saint-Gaudens' sculptural assistants, James Earle Fraser. Saint-Gaudens trusted Fraser's sense of color and his ability to correctly "bronze" the piece after the gilding to achieve the preferred effect.[80] The artist himself was now too ill to undertake the trip.

In 1904, Saint-Gaudens engaged the firm of Casteras Brothers of New York City, to send a man to Buffalo to make a plaster piece mold and cast of the angel. This first mold was unsatisfactory, so in 1905, he asked the Albright Museum to make another mold. The museum hired Joseph Balk of Buffalo, to do the work.[81]

James Earle Fraser recalled that Saint-Gaudens never finished the Shaw to his satisfaction before it was installed in Boston, and that while in Paris he remodeled the angel with the specific intention of cutting it out of the bronze in Boston and replacing it with the final version. At the same time he had talked of repatinating the monument in gold; he saw the early deterioration of the bronze patina. It was toward this end in 1904/5 that Saint-Gaudens had molds made of the angel, but died before he could pursue his idea any further. Later, his widow, Augusta Homer Saint-Gaudens, had a bronze cast made from this mold, and in 1923 sold it to the Brooklyn Museum.

The Albright Knox Art Gallery exhibited the *Shaw Memorial* from 1905 until 1919, at which time the gallery was needed for other exhibitions and a wall was erected in front of the monument. The relief then remained hidden for almost thirty years. In 1945, the Trustees of the Saint-Gaudens Memorial began negotiations to acquire the *Shaw Memorial* cast for the Saint-Gaudens Memorial site in Cornish, New Hampshire. The previous year, the "Studio of the Caryatids" at Cornish burned to the ground, with the loss of many large plaster casts. The Memorial now planned to construct a new exhibition gallery and was anxious to include casts of some of the sculptor's renown public monuments. It was not until January 1949, however, that the Shaw was finally dismantled and shipped to Cornish. Joseph Balk, now age seventy-three, directed the project. He was the same one who dismantled and relocated the relief to the Albright Gallery in 1901.

The Shaw Memorial, fourth plaster version, as it was exhibited at Cornish, NH, 1959-1996.

CORNISH

The cast arrived in Cornish in late January 1949, but because of financial constraints, remained in storage until the summer of 1959. The Memorial trustees mounted a fund raising campaign and the New York firm of Platt Brothers Architects, designed an open protective garden pavilion. Sculptor, John Terken of New York, was hired to install the relief at the end of the "Bowling Green," a long, rectangular garden area enclosed by twelve-foot high hedges. With a hired assistant, Terken worked for fourteen days to piece the monument back together. After ten years in storage, the relief needed extensive restoration, especially along the joints and damaged areas of the base and background. Because of the expense of replicating the gold leaf, the sculpture was instead painted a green color to simulate oxidized bronze. Terken returned in 1962, to make repairs and touch up the surface, damaged somewhat by exposure to the elements.

In 1965, the Trustees of the Saint-Gaudens Memorial donated the site and its collections to the National Park Service, and it became the Saint-Gaudens National Historic Site. Other than occasional minor repairs to the surface, no action was taken with the Shaw Memorial cast until 1981. That year, the National Park Service engaged the Center of Conservation and Technical Services, Fogg Art Museum at Harvard University, to restore the surface patination resembling gilded bronze.

By 1993, it was clear that the plaster cast could no longer remain outdoors without eventually suffering extensive damage because of uncontrolled environmental conditions, especially extreme changes in ambient humidity. The Saint-Gaudens Memorial Trustees, in collaboration with the National Park Service, initiated a campaign to raise funds to replicate the plaster in bronze. The plaster would be conserved and placed on long-term loan to the National Gallery of Art. The Modern Art Foundry of Long Island City, New York, was contracted to cast the bronze from molds made by the Robert Shure, Skylight Studios of Woburn, Massachusetts.

It was fitting that on the one-hundredth anniversary of the *Shaw Memorial's* dedication in Boston, a new bronze cast of the artist's final creative efforts on this masterpiece was unveiled at the Saint-Gaudens National Historic Site in Cornish, New Hampshire, the original plaster was restored and re-erected in the National Gallery of Art, Washington, D.C., with the gilded patina. These events surrounding the Shaw Memorial demonstrate a new appreciation and recognition of both the sculpture and what it signifies. The plaster and the bronze casts of the final, and to the sculptor's mind, perfected, version of this great monument will now be seen and enjoyed by generations to come.

ACKNOWLEDGEMENTS

Many individuals assisted with their time, suggestions, and research on this project. I would especially like to thank the following for their help: the staff at Special Collections, Dartmouth College Library, William Loos, Buffalo Central Library, Rare Books & Manuscript Division, the staff at Special Collections, Syracuse University Library, Catherine L. Mason, Erie County Historical Society, Janice Lurie, Albright Knox Art Gallery, Maureen Melton, Boston Museum of Fine Arts, Ann Wheeler, National Cowboy Hall of Fame, Robert Jaccaud, Dartmouth College Library, Judith N. Lund, New Bedford Whaling Museum, Susan Greendyke Lachevre, Massachusetts Art Commission, Elizabeth Ajemian, Joyce Schiller, Diane P. Fischer, Elizabeth Krawczyk, James Percoco, Lawrence Nowlan, Bridgid Sullivan, Carol Warner, Clifford Crane, Don Wickman, Edwin Quiroz and Gia Lane.

ENDNOTES

1. Burchard, Peter, *One Gallant Rush: Robert Gould Shaw and His Brave Black Regiment*, New York; St. Martin's Press, 1965, p. 57

2. Craig, Tom, *Colored Volunteer*, Sheet Music, Philadelphia, 1863, Broadsides Collection, John Hay Library, Brown University

3. Burchard, p. 94

4. Emilio, Luis F., *A Brave Black Regiment: History of the Fifty-Fourth Regiment of Massachusetts Volunteer Infantry 1863-1865*: Boston; Boston Book Company, 1894, p. 392

5. Ibid., p. 72 The Union records referred to Wagner as a fort, while technically it was an artillery battery, and so called by the Confederate army.

6. Ibid., p. 78

7. Ibid., p. 82

8. Brown, William Wells, *The Negro in the American Rebellion: His Heroism and his Fidelity*, Boston; Lee & Shepard, 1867, p.201

9. Cox, Clinton, *Undying Glory: The Story of the Massachusetts 54th Regiment*, New York; Scholastic, Inc. 1991, p. 96

10. Emilio, p. 95

11. Hine, Darlene Clark, ed. *Black Women in America: An Historical Encyclopedia*, Brooklyn, Carlson Publishing Inc., 1993, p. 1179

12. Emilio, p. 99 Shaw's personal effects, including his gold watch and sash, were reportedly taken from the body by one of the garrison troops. After the war, Shaw's sword was acquired by a Confederate officer who returned it to the family.

13. Emilio, p. 102-103

14. Emilio, p. 103

15. Wade, Hugh Mason, *A Brief History of Cornish, 1763-1974*, Hanover; University Press of New England, 1976, p.38

16. Emilio, p. 94

17. During the war the Fifty-Fourth had a total enrollment of 1,354. Of these, five officers and ninety-five men were confirmed killed in action, or died of their wounds. Another fifty-seven were listed as missing, of which nineteen were later reported to have died in prison. Thirty others were captured and later exchanged or released at the end of the war. Twenty officers and 274 men were wounded, and another seventy-five succumbed to disease. In all, the regiment suffered 500 casualties, a rate of over 36%.

    In 1996, the Civil War Soldiers and Sailors project created a computerized data bank listing all known names of men in the United States Colored Troops. These names are available for searching through the Internet. Eventually the names of all Union and Confederate soldiers and sailors will be placed into this databank.

18. Kirstein, Lincoln, *Lay This Laurel: New York;* Eakins Press, 1973

19. Emilio, p.102-103

20. *The Monument to Robert Gould Shaw: Its Inception, Completion and Unveiling 1865-1897*: Boston; Houghton Mifflin and Co., 1897, p.1

21. Ibid., p.8

22. Edward Atkison Papers, Massachusetts Historical Society, Boston, Massachusetts, Letter from Augustus Saint-Gaudens to Edward Atkinson, December 5, 1882.

23. Ibid., Letter October 3, 1883, from Augustus Saint-Gaudens to Edward Atkinson.

24. The Papers of Augustus Saint-Gaudens, Special Collections, Dartmouth College Library, Hanover, New Hampshire. Contract between Saint-Gaudens and the Shaw Memorial Committee.

25. Saint-Gaudens, Homer, ed. *The Reminiscences of Augustus Saint-Gaudens,* New York; The Century Co., 1913, v. I, p. 332

26. Ibid., v. I, p. 332

27. Atkinson Papers, Letter from Augustus Saint-Gaudens to Edward Atkinson, March 19, 1883

28. Letter from Augusta Saint-Gaudens to Augustus Saint-Gaudens, September 2, 1883. The Papers of Augustus Saint-Gaudens, Special Collections, Baker Library, Dartmouth College, Hanover, New Hampshire

29. Dartmouth, Letter from Augustus Saint-Gaudens to Eugenie Nichols. See also, Marcus, Lois Goldreich, "The Shaw Memorial by Augustus Saint-Gaudens: A History Painting in Bronze," *Winterthur Portfolio*, v. XIV, No. I, pp 1-24. This painting is now in the D'Orsey Museum in Paris.

30. Saint-Gaudens, v. I, p. 333

31. Ibid., v. I, pp. 337-338. There is no record of whether these men ever posed for Saint-Gaudens, and none of the other models' names are known. None of the models were actual veterans of the 54th Regiment. Of the forty study heads originally created only six are known and are in the collections of Saint-Gaudens National Historic Site.

32. Dartmouth, Letter from Augustus Saint-Gaudens to Gaeton Ardisson, November 14, 1897

33. Saint-Gaudens, v.I, pp. 343-343

34. Autobiography, manuscript. The Papers of James Earle Fraser, Special Collections, Syracuse University, Syracuse, New York

35. Saint-Gaudens, v. I, p. 343

36. Ibid., v. I, p. 333. Sculptors sometimes made casts of a model's body especially if it was a difficult pose. Saint-Gaudens made casts of model, Julia "Dodie" Baird, who posed for the body of the *Diana*, since the stance was tiring to hold for more than a few minutes at a time.

37. Atkinson Papers, Letter from Augustus Saint-Gaudens, January 20, 1891.

38. Ibid., Letter from Augustus Saint-Gaudens, February 11, 1893

39. Kirstein

40. Wilkinson, p.282

41. Letter from Charles F. McKim to Augustus Saint-Gaudens, Box #I, late 1894, Charles Follen McKim Papers, Library of Congress, Washington, D.C.

42. Saint-Gaudens, v. 2, p. 78-79

43. Ibid., v. 2, p.88

44. Atkinson Papers, Letter Augustus Saint-Gaudens, February 21, 1897

45. Dartmouth, Letter from the City of Boston Art Commission to Augustus Saint-Gaudens, December 9, 1898

46. Atkinson Papers, Letter from Lizzie Nichols to her husband?, August, 1895

47. Ibid., Letter from Augustus Saint-Gaudens, December 31, 1895

48. Ibid., Letter from Augustus Saint-Gaudens, May 8, 1896

49. Edward Atkinson Letterbooks, MHS, Letter from Edward Atkinson to Augustus Saint-Gaudens, June 5, 1896

50. Wilkinson, p. 284

51. Ibid., p. 284

52. Coffin, William A., "The Shaw Memorial And the Sculptor St. Gaudens," *Century Illustrated Magazine*, v. XXXII, June, 1897 p. 176-177, 179-186, 194-200. Once the changes were made, other photographs of the relief were taken after the unveiling. A doctored photograph also appeared in a Harpers Weekly issue just prior to the unveiling. In this, the 1896 photo was used but the angel cut out and replaced with the version used in the bronze. This was all done without Saint-Gaudens consent and he was quite angered over the affair.

53. Saint-Gaudens, v. I, p. 344

54. Though Homer Saint-Gaudens refers to this as a laurel branch, Augustus himself, calls it an olive branch.

55. Saint-Gaudens, v. I, p. 344

56. Nichols, Rose Standish, "Familiar Letters of Augustus Saint-Gaudens," *McClure's Magazine*, v. XXXI, October, 1908, No. 6, pp. 603-616, Letter from Augustus Saint-Gaudens to Rose Nichols, February 17, 1897

Rose Nichols was the daughter of Augusta Homer Saint-Gaudens' sister, Marian. She was a landscape designer and owned a house in Cornish not far from the Saint-Gaudens home. Her former home in Boston is now the Nichols House Museum.

57. Saint-Gaudens, v. I, p. 343
58. Rose Nichols, Letter from Augustus Saint-Gaudens to Rose Nichols, February 17, 1897
59. James Earle Fraser Papers. Autobiography
60. Ibid.
61. McKim Papers. Letter from Charles F. McKim to Augustus Saint-Gaudens, September 3, 1896
62. Wilkinson, p. 285
63. Monument, p. 47
64. Ibid., p. 60
65. Saint-Gaudens, v. 2, p. 83
66. Ibid., v. 2, p. 84
67. Monument, p. 84
68. Kirstein, p.78
69. Saint-Gaudens, v. 2, p. 94
70. Gilchrist, Marianne McLeod, "The Shaw Family of Staten Island: Elizabeth Gaskell's American Friends," *The Gaskell Society Journal*, v. IX, 1995, pp. I-I2. Mrs. Shaw died in Boston in 1907 and is buried in Lenox, Mass The Haggerty family owned a house in Lenox and it was here that the Shaws spent their honeymoon.
71. Monument, p. 60
72. Saint-Gaudens, v. I, p. 347
73. Museum Archives, The Museum of Fine Arts, Boston, Massachusetts. Saint-Gaudens arranged with the Director, Mr. Loring, to have "Chico," the museum's packer go to the sculptor's New York studio in December, 1897, to pack and ship the Shaw cast to Paris.
74. An article in the 1898 *Gazette des Beaux Arts* also mentioned that the twenty-third was the date of the battle. By 1898, Saint-Gaudens apparently had forgotten the actual date and used this by mistake.
75. Dartmouth, Saint-Gaudens papers, "Reminiscences of Augustus Saint-Gaudens" by William Coffin
76. Ibid., Letter from Augustus Saint-Gaudens to John M. Beatty, Carnegie Institute, March 31, 1904
77. Ibid., Letter from Augustus Saint-Gaudens to William A. Coffin, November 2, 1901
78. Ibid., Plaster casts sent to the foundry are not destroyed during the casting process. The original

plaster for the bronze in Boston was returned to Saint-Gaudens from the Gorham Company Foundry and shipped to Cornish.
79. James Earle Fraser Papers.
80. Dartmouth, Saint-Gaudens Papers, Letter from Edward B. Green to Augustus Saint-Gaudens, July, 1905
81. Ibid., Letter from Augustus Saint-Gaudens to Albright Art Gallery

BIBLIOGRAPHY

Adams, Virginia M. ed. *On the Altar of Freedom: A Black Soldier's Civil War Letters From the Front*; Amherst; University of Massachusetts Press, 1991

Axelrod, Steven, "Colonel Shaw in American Poetry: 'For the Union Dead' and its Precursors," *American Quarterly*, v. XXIV, No. 4, October 1972, pp. 523-537

Blatt, Martin H., Brown, Thomas J., Yacovone, Donald, ed. *Hope & Glory: Essays on the Legacy of the Fifty-Fourth Massachusetts Regiment*, Amherst, University of Massachusetts Press, 2001

Burchard, Peter, *One Gallant Rush: Robert Gould Shaw and His Brave Black Regiment*, New York; St. Martin's Press, 1965

Brown, William Wells, *The Negro in the American Rebellion: His Heroism and his Fidelity*, Boston; Lee & Shepard, 1867

Catalogue of the Exhibition of Fine Arts: Pan American Exposition, Buffalo, 1901, Buffalo; 1901

Coffin, William A., "The Shaw Memorial and the Sculptor St. Gaudens," *Century Illustrated Magazine*, v. XXXII, June, 1897 p. 176-177, 179-186, 194-200

Cox, Clinton, *Undying Glory: The Story of the Massachusetts 54th Regiment*, New York; Scholastic, Inc. 1991

Dryfhout, John H. *The Work of Augustus Saint-Gaudens*, Hanover; University Press of New England, 1982

Duncan, Russell, ed. *Blue-Eyed Child of Fortune: The Civil War Letters of Colonel Robert Gould Shaw*, Athens; The University of Georgia Press, 1992

Emilio, Luis F., *A Brave Black Regiment: History of the Fifty-Fourth Regiment of Massachusetts Volunteer Infantry 1863-1865*: Boston; Boston Book Company, 1894

Gilchrist, Marianne McLeod, "The Shaw Family of Staten Island: Elizabeth Gaskell's American Friends," *The Gaskell Society Journal*, v. IX, 1995, pp. 1-12

Hanson, Chadwick, The 54th Massachusetts Volunteer Black Infantry as a Subject for American Artists, The *Massachusetts Review*, v. XVI, Autumn 1975, pp. 759

Hine, Darlene Clark, ed. *Black Women in America: An Historical Encyclopedia*, Brooklyn, Carlson Publishing Inc., 1993

de Hureaux, Alain Daguerre, *Augustus Saint-Gaudens 1848-1907: A Master of American Sculpture*, Paris, Somogy Editions D'Art, 1999

Kirstein, Lincoln, *Lay This Laurel:* New York; Eakins Press, 1973

Lucas, Justin, "Le Salon Des Salons (1898): Art et Critique," *Revue Encyclopedique,* No. 252, 2 Juillet 1898, pp. 600-603

The Monument to Robert Gould Shaw: Its Inception, Completion and Unveiling 1865-1897, Boston; Houghton Mifflin and Co., 1897

Marcus, Lois Goldreich, "The Shaw Memorial by Augustus Saint-Gaudens: A History Painting in Bronze," *Winterthur Portfolio*, v. XIV, No. 1, pp 1-24

Nichols, Rose Standish, "Familiar Letters of Augustus Saint-Gaudens," *McClure's Magazine*, v. XXXI, October, 1908, No. 6, pp. 603-616

Saint-Gaudens, Homer, ed. *The Reminiscences of Augustus Saint-Gaudens*, New York; The Century Co., 1913

Thompson, Joann Marie, *The Art and Architecture of the Pan-American Exposition*, Buffalo, New York, 1901. Ph.D. dissertation, Rutgers University, New Brunswick, N.J., 1980

Wade, Hugh Mason, *A Brief History of Cornish, 1763-1974*, Hanover; University Press of New England, 1976, p.38

Walton, W., *Exposition Universelle, 1900: The Chefs-D'oeuvre*, Philadelphia; George Barrie & Son, Publishers, 1900

Wilkinson, Burke, *Uncommon Clay: The Life and Works of Augustus Saint-Gaudens*, San Diego; Harcourt Brace Jovanovich, 1985

Wilson, Joseph T., *The Black Phalanx: A History of the Negro Soldiers of the United States in the Wars of 1775-1812, 1861-65*, Hartford; American Publishing Company, 1888

Yacavone, Donald, ed., *A Voice of Thunder: The Civil War Letters of George E. Stephens*, Urbana; University of Illinois Press, 1996

MANUSCRIPTS

Albright Knox Gallery, Buffalo, New York, Museum Archives

Archives of American Art, Smithsonian Institution, Washington, D.C., various collections

Dartmouth College, Hanover, New Hampshire, Special Collections, The Papers of Augustus Saint-Gaudens and The Papers of the Trustees of the Saint-Gaudens Memorial

Library of Congress, Washington, D.C., Charles Follen McKim Papers

Massachusetts Historical Society, Boston, Massachusetts, Luis F. Emilio Collection and Atkinson Family Papers

The Museum of Fine Arts, Boston, Massachusetts, Museum Archives, Papers of General Loring

Schlesinger Library, Radcliffe College, Cambridge, Massachusetts, Emerson-Nichols Papers

Syracuse University, Syracuse, New York, Special Collections, The Papers of James Earle Fraser

OMNIA RELIQVIT
SERVARE REMPVBLICAM

NER JVLY TWENTY THIRD EIGHTEEN HVNDRED AND SIXTY THREE

MEMORIAL

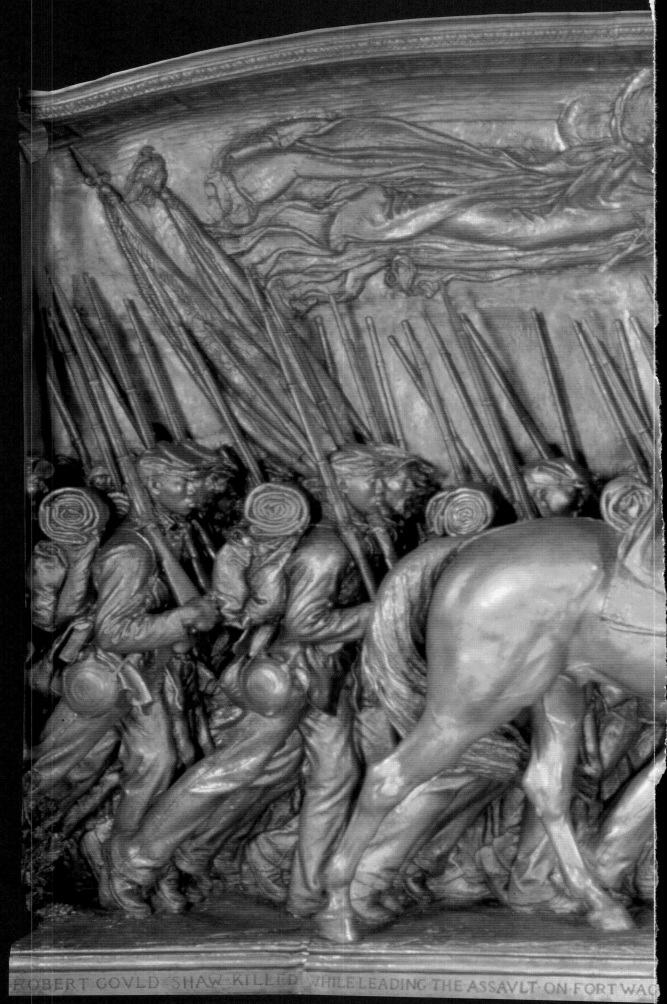

ROBERT GOVLD SHAW KILLED WHILE LEADING THE ASSAVLT ON FORT WAG

THE SHAW

First version plaster, October 1896.

Third version plaster, April 1898.

Second version bronze, May 1897. (Boston, MA)

Fourth, and final, version patinated plaster, April 1900. (Cornish, NH)

Unveiling of the bronze cast of the Shaw Memorial, July 13, 1997.
Saint-Gaudens National Historic Site, Cornish, New Hampshire.

A COMMEMORATION:
THE SHAW MEMORIAL AS AMERICAN CULTURE

by Ludwig Lauerhass

The American journey has not ended.
America is never accomplished.
America is always still to build.
     —*Archibald MacLeish*

And the crown is as bright o'er the sable
brows as over the golden hair.
     —*George H. Boker*

Like those mighty oaks that from tiny acorns grow, national epics often stem from events that are small in their own right, and it may take years for their transcendent message to be fully grasped by the national imagination. Such was the case of the assault on Fort Wagner, South Carolina, July 18, 1863, by the Fifty-Fourth Massachusetts Volunteers under the command of Colonel Robert Gould Shaw. Although the attack failed and the regiment quickly withdrew after sustaining heavy casualties, the gallantry of its African American troops and the heroic death of its youthful Boston Brahmin commanding officer received immediate notice in the press and set in motion reverberations that have been felt to this day. The Fifty-Fourth's symbolic value had, in fact, been foreordained. If not the first, it was the preeminent all-black regiment, albeit officered mostly by whites, to be formed in the Civil War and was intended to show the effectiveness of blacks as fighting men and, more broadly, to prove their manhood. The regiment became a metaphor for emancipa-

After the unveiling, May 31, 1897. Boston, Massachusetts. Courtesy Boston Public Library.

tion born in a baptism of fire. Then, from an early commemoration by James Russell Lowell, "Memoriae Positum, R.G.S., 1863" published in the *Atlantic Monthly* (January 1864)[1] through its most recent in the film *Glory*[2] released in 1989, the march of its symbolic portrayal has moved from an originally limited Bostonian and Union context to its ultimate recognition as the basis of an American epic, embodying our fundamental values and continuing aspirations of equality and liberty.

Despite the widespread contemporary reportage of the event for its propaganda effect and its sporadic precursory commemorations, the continuing march of the epic was not assured until the sculptor Augustus Saint-Gaudens captured the essence of its meaning with aesthetic power and

a

b

c

d

e

f

g

moral conviction in his memorial to Robert Gould Shaw and the men of the Fifty-Fourth (see illustration). Since its dedication one hundred years ago on Decoration (Memorial) Day 1897, this unforgettably moving bronze monument has given the epic both permanence and prominence in its Boston Common location near one of the cradles of the American Republic. Without this constantly viewed reminder, the significance of the Fifty-Fourth might gradually have faded as a memory of an ever more distant war. Moreover, this monument was singular in its recognition of the contributions made by African American soldiers and of blacks and whites fighting together in support of national values. It would be hard to exaggerate the importance of the Shaw Memorial and its role in the epic making process. From the time of its unveiling, the centennial of which we celebrated in 1997, the monument has sustained our common vision of the epic. Future echoes of the theme were to hark back to this intense sculptural expression, reflecting upon it and drawing inspiration from it, as much as from the wartime event itself. In this sense, the artist Saint-Gaudens has served as the Homer of the Fifty-Fourth and of the Civil War.

The march of the Fifty-Fourth as epic had actually begun before the end of the war. The event began its transfiguration into poetry not long after the dramatic Fort Wagner assault, and its retelling in the arts has continued to this day. The epic has had its ebb and flow of interest, as did the history of the event itself. As time passed, reportage yielded to historiography, and aesthetic expression was manifested in an ever-expanding range of art forms and genres—poetry, essay, prints, sculpture, photographs, film and television. There was also interplay among them—poem harking back to poem, monument displaying verse, essay explaining sculpture, monument inspiring poem, poem prefac-

The unveiling ceremony, Boston, May 31, 1897; photographs taken by Augusta Saint-Gaudens using a Kodak box camera.
a. Before the unveiling; flag draped monument
b. The unveiling
c-d. Veterans of the 54th regiment
e. Veterans of the 5th Cavalry of Massachusetts (?)
f. 1st Corps of Cadets, Massachusetts Volunteer Militia
g. Light Battery A, Massachusetts Volunteer Militia

Photographs 2 x 2¾ in. Collection, U.S. Department of Interior, National Park Service, Saint-Gaudens NHS.

ing symphonic piece, sculpture glossing film, and criticism entwined with all. Immediate reactions came during the war, and occasional commemorations followed over the next few years. The animating vision in the march of the epic came with the dedication of the Shaw Memorial by Augustus Saint-Gaudens in 1897 and the outpouring of expression which surrounded it. A later series of variations on the theme came with the Civil War Centennial in the early 1960s, and yet another in the late 1980s and 90s, spurred on by another revival of interest in the war and in the field of African American history, culminating with *Glory* and *The Civil War* series. Although commonly, if not always, the product of cultural elites, versions of the epic have succeeded in broadening their appeal to reach mass popular audiences.

Perhaps the first voice sounding an epic tone for the Regiment was that of a private in Company A. The sentiments expressed here in a song, published early in 1863 in the *Boston Transcript,* preceded the engagement in battle but were later justified by the heroism at Fort Wagner.

> McClellan went to Richmond with two hundred thousand brave:
> He said, 'keep back the niggers,' and the Union he would save.
> Little Mac he had his way, still the Union is in tears:
> *Now* they call for the help of the colored volunteers.

❨

> So rally, boys, rally, let us never mind the past:
> We had a hard road to travel, but our day is coming fast;
> For God is for the right, and we have no need to fear:
> The Union must be saved by the colored volunteer.
> *Chorus*—Oh! Give us a flag all free without a slave,
> We'll fight to defend It as our fathers did so brave:
> The gallant Comp'ny A will make the rebels dance,
> And we'll stand by the Union, if we only have a chance.[3]

This would seem to indicate that enlisted soldiers from the Regiment's rank and file also believed in the special mission of the Fifty-Fourth and that they accepted the challenge. By their acts they hoped to help to save the day for the Union and to join in the mainstream of history with those who had defended it in the past.

In the aftermath of battle, the meanings and ironies of the sacrifice were expressed in many forms and on varying cultural levels. One of the most cogent depictions is found in a poem written shortly after the assault on

Fort Wagner by George H. Boker.

> "They buried him with his niggers!"
>   Together they fought and died
>
> There was room for them all where they laid him
>   (The grave was deep and wide)
>
> For his beauty and youth and valor,
>   Their patience and love and pain;
>
> And at the last day together
>   They shall be found again.
>
>   ☾
>
> "They buried him with his niggers!"
>   But the glorious souls set free
>
> Are leading the van of the army
>   That fights for liberty
>
> Brothers in death, in glory
>   The same palm branches bear;
>
> And the crown is as bright o'er the sable brows
>   As over the golden hair. [4]
>
> They were together in life, in death, and in glory.

Pictorial views of the assault on Fort Wagner, either in sketches or photographs, illustrated contemporary accounts in newspapers and magazines. Wood engravings of the attack and a portrait of Shaw along with an obituary, "The Late Colonel Shaw," appeared in *Harper's Weekly.* Other pictorials were issued as separate prints of the type popularized by Currier and Ives as were many photographic portraits of the Fifty-Fourth's officers and men—some of which were later reproduced in Luis Emilio's official regimental history.[5] One of these was of Sergeant William H. Carney of Company C who gained fame, and ultimately the Congressional Medal of Honor, for his successful efforts to save the national colors during the battle. In the photograph, used as frontispiece for the history, he is shown holding the flag with a caption identifying it as the one he saved at Wagner and quoting Carney, "The old flag never touched the ground, boys." This story inspired a sculptor, Truman Howe Bartlett, to inquire about Carney's exploits, saying that he "would make a splendid subject for a statuette." Colonel Hallowell replied with a verbal description: "Sergt. Carney was an African, of I should think full blood; of very limited education, but very intelligent; bright face, lips and nose (comparatively) finely cut, head rather round, skin very dark, height about five feet eight inches, not very athletic or muscular; had lived in New Bedford, Mass., for many years." If a "statuette" was ever completed on the basis of this description, it obviously would not have been an accurate personal likeness. It can be assumed that most contemporary illustrations conveyed a certain symbolic representation of truth rather than historical accuracy.[6]

That Shaw himself would come to personify the gallantry of the Regiment was to be expected. Not only was he its commander, but coming as he did from an exalted station in society, he received a high level of attention and respect for his sacrifice. His heroic death was held as both a personal and family loss and as a moral contribution of Boston and Harvard to the preservation of the Union and the redemption of the colored race. The epic process in this vein enlisted the best New England literary talent, including Ralph Waldo Emerson and James Russell Lowell who were personal friends of the Shaw family. Lowell's "Memoriæ Positum, R.G.S., 1863" was the first major poem to focus on the nobility of Shaw's death in the prime of his youth and its transcendent significance for the nation. While the tone is intensely personal, the ode ends with a salute to the land which produced such dedication.

> Brave, good, and true,
> I see him stand before me now.
>
> ❆
>
> Right in the van,
> On the red rampart's slippery swell,
> With heart that beat a charge, he fell
>   Forward, as fits a man;
> But the high soul burns on to light men's feet
> Where death for noble ends makes dying sweet;
>
> ❆
>
> His life's expense
> Hath won for him coeval youth
> With immaculate prime of Truth;
>
> ❆
>
> Ah, when the fight is won,
> Dear Land, whom triflers now make bold to scorn
> (Thee! from whose forehead Earth awaits her morn!)
>   How nobler shall the sun
> Flame in the sky, how braver breathe the air,
> That thou bred'st children who for thee could dare
>   And die as thine have done![7]

In sculpture, a bust of Colonel Shaw was completed before the war's end by Edmonia Lewis. She was born of a African American father and a Chippewa mother, and had received formal training as a sculptor in Boston through the influence of the abolitionist leader William Lloyd Garrison. The bust of Shaw was praised by critics and, as reproduced in plaster copies, achieved a modest commercial success. It also launched a successful career for the artist who went on to work in Rome and to produce a number of studies on Indian themes as well as one of a slave man and woman rejoicing at the news of emancipation.[8]

Although planning for a great monument commemorating both Shaw's personal gallantry and the symbolic heroism of the Fifty-Fourth began in late 1865, the final memorial, brilliantly executed by the New York sculptor Augustus Saint-Gaudens, the foremost commemorative sculptor of his day, was not completed and dedicated until 1897. The original fund-raising committee, chaired by governor John Andrew himself, included Senator Charles Sumner and the poet Henry Wadsworth Longfellow. By 1883 the fund had reached more than $16,000, and Augustus Saint-Gaudens was contracted to undertake the project in the following year. The artist devoted parts of the next twelve years to completion of what was to become his greatest work. The noted architect Charles Follen McKim designed the pedestal, benches, and stone frame into which the bronze sculpture was placed.

The life-sized monument is a simple metaphoric statement of what the war was ultimately about, white and black together under arms marching into battle to preserve the Union, to emancipate the slaves, and to lead the nation, as Lincoln put it, to a new birth of freedom. At the center of the sculpture, Colonel Shaw is portrayed on horseback, drawn sword in hand, riding at the side of a group of his black soldiers who are marching in columns four abreast with shouldered muskets and colors rising well above the level of the men. At the far right a drummer boy is in the lead, and above them all floats an angel on her divine mission urging them forward. The overall impression made by the figures is one of realism. Even the angel seems lifelike. While each figure is notably individual in appearance and expression, together they convey a sense of resolve and common purpose, marching to fulfill their destiny. Based on photographs and other portraits, the likeness of Shaw is historically accurate. For the drummer boy and soldiers Saint-Gaudens relied on models chosen from blacks available in New York City to serve as types that he wished to portray, as he did in the case of the angel. The net result is striking in its verisimilitude, a forceful and well-crafted expression of the monument's symbolic meaning.

The memorial is also replete with verbal messages. Cast within the bronze between the troops and the angel's arm is the inscription *Omnia relinquit servare rempublicam* (He leaves everything behind to save the republic), motto of the Society of the Cincinnati, a fraternal, patriotic organization formed by the regular officers at the end of the Revolutionary War. Below, on the pedestal, is the dedication to Robert Gould Shaw, Colonel of the Fifty-Fourth Massachusetts Infantry, followed by a stanza from the 1864 Lowell poem "Right in the van." Other inscriptions are on the back of the monument, including the homage of Harvard's President Charles W. Eliot.

Artistically, the monument is within its genre the greatest American achievement of its day and arguably the finest piece of memorial sculpture ever produced in this country. Augustus Saint-Gaudens masterfully captured the spirit of his times and projected it in sculpted form. Sculpture, especially on a large commemorative scale, came to enhance our public space, as did parks, squares, government buildings, libraries, museums, and concert halls in the period from 1876 to 1917 recalled as the American Renaissance.[11] It was the era of the "City Beautiful" movement when one international exposition followed another, and the need was felt to express national identity and pride symbolically through works of art and architecture. The grand traditions of the Italian Renaissance provided models, and Saint-Gaudens like many of his contemporary artists had been strongly influenced by them during years of apprenticeship in Rome and study at the École des Beaux-Arts in Paris. Standard elements of Renaissance iconography including the equestrian presentation of Shaw and even the form of a guiding angel were well suited to this monument and were the types of images that the viewing public had come to expect. Saint-Gaudens' collaborator Charles McKim also held to the values of the Renaissance, in his execution of this memorial, in much of his architectural work, and in his founding of the American Academy of Rome.

Aesthetically, the monument's impact has been profound from the outset. Writing in the *Century Magazine* shortly after the dedication ceremonies in 1897, William A. Coffin described the work in all of its detail and concluded, "How unified and complete it is! With what force is the general effect brought to one, making him feel the grandeur of the whole! . . . No poet's dream of heroism, glory, or devotion . . . could be realized in material form as this is . . . this beautiful work of art."[12] Another contemporary critic Lorado Taft, as noted by a later art historian Albert Boime, thought it was "one of the most impressive monuments of modern time," and compared Saint-Gaudens's treatment of the upraised, shouldered muskets with that of lances in Velasquez's "Surrender at Breda." He was especially struck by the realistic sense of marching conveyed by the bronze figures, " The movement of this great composition is extraordinary. We almost hear the roll of the drums and the shuflle of heavy shoes. It makes the day of that brave departure very real again." It is "the fit expression of America's new-born patriotism."[13] A few years later, a black art historian, Freeman Murray, praised the work of Saint-Gaudens for "instinct with taste and technical mastery, yet sublime in its expressiveness and mighty in its moving power."[14]

Nearly a century later its power to evoke an emotional response is undiminished. In a recent biography of Saint-Gaudens, Burke Wilkinson describes the Shaw Memorial as a "Symphony in Bronze." . . . There is so much variety to it, from the delicate bas-relief of the hovering angel to the high relief of many of the marching men, to the full statue-in-the-round quality of the Colonel and his charger, that no other musical analogy would be accurate. To carry the comparison one step further . . . musically speaking the instruction under which the sculptor composed his symphony was *nobilmente* . . .[15] The combining of the techniques of full round, high relief and bas-relief, may also be thought of as the artist's separate treatment of Shaw as portrait, the soldiers as realistic but representative types, and the angel as allegory—the closer to historical accuracy, the fuller the sculptural form the same tripartite division may be seen to represent yet another separation—of underlying purpose, Shaw's devotion to duty and sense of noblesse oblige, the patriotic and self-fulfilling sense of manhood on the part of the troops, and the angel's expression of divine message.

The symbolic representation was most apt and the commemoration complete. It all needed to be there: Shaw, his men, and the sense of mission. An equestrian statue of Shaw alone, as Saint-Gaudens had originally conceived the monument, would have been pretentious. Unlike General Sherman, another of the sculptor's subjects, the young colonel was not sufficiently heroic in his own right, and his military contribution to the war had been slight. Shaw's family was correct in insisting that the memorial should include the men of the Fifty-Fourth, since the sacrifice at Fort Wagner had meaning only in martyrdom of blacks and whites fighting and dying for one another. While the figure of Shaw on his horse is central to the composition, he is there to lead his men as liberators of their race. They are mutually dependent. The beckoning angel is needed to complete the metaphoric message that the march of the two together toward equality must continue, that victory still lies ahead, that the new birth of freedom envisioned by Lincoln has yet to be achieved.

Long anticipated, well planned, and dramatically executed, the dedication of the Shaw Memorial finally came about on Decoration Day, May 31, 1897. It amounted to no less than a gala civic celebration engaging the elite of Boston and veterans of the war in a final consecration of Shaw as local hero and of the Fifty-Fourth Regiment as the ultimate symbol of the state's Union patriotism and moral virtue. The monument would stand as a perpetual reminder of this sacrifice, becoming a part of Bostonian elite lore. The ceremonies began on Boston Common with the unveiling of the statue and a few words by Governor Roger Wolcott, followed by a twenty-one gun salute and a military parade including sixty-five veterans of the Fifty-Fourth which passed before the reviewing stand constructed on the steps of the Statehouse across the street from the monument.[16] Here they marched in life for the last time in the same spot that they had earlier with Colonel Shaw on May 28, 1863, when going off to war and under Colonel Hallowell, who had assumed command of the Regiment on Shaw's death, on September 2, 1865, upon their triumphal homecoming. From this day on, their march continued only in the realms of reconstructed image and historical memory.

That night an extended commemoration in honor of the Brotherhood of Man rounded out the festivities. The Boston *Evening Transcript* of June 1 captured the emotional tone of the moment "in the flag-filled, enthusiasm-warmed patriotic and glowing atmosphere of Music Hall, people felt keenly that here was the justification of the old abolition spirit of Massachussetts . . . The scene was full of historic beauty and a deep significance 'Cold Boston' was alive with the fire that is always hot in her heart for righteousness and truth. . . . Battle music had filled the air. Ovation after ovation, applause warm and prolonged had greeted the officers and friends of Colonel Shaw, the sculptor Saint-Gaudens, the memorial committee. The governor and the Negro soldiers of the Fifty-Fourth. . . ." Later, that evening's principal speaker, Booker T. Washington, recalled the crowd's height of exuberance which came as he extolled the bravery of Sergeant Carney who in turn then rose to his feet and waved the tattered flag which he had carried at Fort Wagner and never allowed to touch the ground. "In dramatic effect I have never seen nor experienced anything that equaled the impression made on the audience. . . . For a good many minutes the audience seemed to entirely lose control of itself and patriotic feeling was at a high pitch.[17] The other major address of the night, given by William James, whose brother Wilkie had served in the Fifty-Fourth, complemented the sentiments offered by Washington. In fact, the two had corresponded earlier in order to coordinate their efforts and avoid duplication.[18] Both, however, developed similar themes, beginning with praise for Shaw and the Fifty-Fourth, then turning to the lessons to be learned from their heroic sacrifice and the goals left to be fulfilled.

In this speech and in an article published two weeks later in *Leslie's Weekly Illustrated,* Booker T. Washington stressed that "it would be hard for any white man to appreciate to what extent the negro race reveres and idolizes the name of Colonel Shaw. Not so much for what he did as for the principle for which he stood . . . Shaw succeeded in making the negro a soldier because he had faith in him as a man." Going beyond personal eulogy, Washington added that "the full measure of the fruit of Fort Wagner and all that this monument stands for will not be realized until every man covered with a black skin shall by patient and natural effort, grow to that height in industry, property, intelligence and moral responsibility, where no man in all our land will be tempted to degrade himself by withholding from his black brother any opportunity which he himself would possess. Until that time comes, the monument will stand for effort, not victory complete. What these heroic souls of the 54th regiment began we must complete . . . in the public school, industrial school, and college . . . most of it must be completed in the effort of the Negro himself . . ." He concluded with a call to realize:

> The slave's chain and the master's alike broken;
>
> The one curse of the race held both in tether;
>
> They are rising, all are rising—
>
> The black and the white together.

White and black, southerner and northerner, and men from all sectors of society would need to work together to achieve the realities of liberty and equality.[19]

For William James the story of Shaw and his Regiment could be read from the monument in "the mingling of elements which the sculptor's genius has brought vividly before the eye. There on foot go the dark outcasts, so true to nature that one can almost hear them breathing as they march . . . warm-blooded champions of a better day for man. There on horseback . . . sits the blue-eyed child of fortune, upon whose happy youth every happy divinity had smiled. Onward they move together, a single resolution kindled in their eyes and animating their otherwise so different frames." For James, Shaw and his comrades showed that Americans of all complexions could fight and die as brothers in order to preserve what he called our American religion, the belief that all men should live in liberty. Slavery had been a perversion of this principle and had to be rooted out. The Shaw monument, then, would serve as a permanent "inciter" to perform similar unselfish public deeds. It would stand as a call for "civic courage," and the lessons of the war were the need to maintain a constant vigil against internal enemies that would undermine the republic. Democracy was still on trial and depended on the functioning of two common civic habits—respect for the opposition party when it fairly wins elections and an unwillingness to tolerate a breach of the public peace. James concluded by urging his countrymen, "Southern and Northern, brothers hereafter, masters, slaves, and enemies no more . . ." to preserve these heirlooms. Our country would then continue "like the city of promise and the ways of all nations be lit up by its light."[20] Thus, James had gone beyond his initial focus on the monument and the story of Shaw and the Fifty-Fourth to a general call for civic virtue, much as Booker T. Washington had shifted from monument and event to a call for Negro self-improvement. This was a pattern that would be repeated.

The Shaw memorial became more than the centerpiece of this commemoration and of the revived interest in the Fifty-Fourth during the 1890s. It was to transcend community pride of Boston and the symbolism of Harvard's achievement as expressed on the eve of the ceremonies, May 30, 1897, when Major Henry Lee Higginson concluded his commemorative address to students of Harvard University and men of the Grand Army of the Republic with:

> In yonder cloister, on the tablet with his classmates of 1860 is engraved the name of Robert Gould Shaw He will always be an heroic figure for you . . .
> Harvard students: whenever you hear of Colonel Shaw, or of any officer or of any man of the 54th Massachusetts Regiment, salute him in the name of Harvard University and Harvard men.[21]

Ironically, Saint-Gaudens' long-delayed completion of the monument meant that the exuberant dedication ceremonies occurred in times that were becoming ever less sympathetic to the ideals which they proclaimed. The sense of commitment to Negro equality which had characterized the post-Civil War days and the era of reconstruction had long since waned. The fervor of Boston that Decoration Day of 1897, was that of a locally confined enclave and hardly expressive of the nationally held sentiments of the day. This was a new and radically different era. Internally, it was a time of Jim Crow laws and of the Supreme Court's *Plessy vs. Ferguson* decision that would validate them for more than a half century. It was a time for the resurgence of the Ku Klux Klan, and the number of lynchings reached record levels—1,226 between 1892 and 1898.

Among those who would become increasingly disenchanted with the post-Reconstruction trends in race relations was the Harvard Ph.D and black historian, W.E.B. DuBois. In a poignant article, "Strivings of the Negro People," published in Boston's *Atlantic Monthly* in August 1897, scarcely three months following the Shaw celebrations, he asked, "Why did God make me an outcast and a stranger in mine own house?" and lamented the sense of two-ness always felt by his race? "An American and a Negro: two souls, two thoughts, two unreconciled strivings, two warring ideals in one dark body." The promise of emancipation had not been kept. "The freedman is not yet fully free, but the Negro hopes for a higher synthesis of civilization and humanity, a true progress with work, culture, and liberty, not singly but together in order to pursue the greater ideals of the American republic." Then in his *Souls of Black Folks,* DuBois argued for "the right to vote, civic equality, and the education of youth according to ability." He concluded with an appeal: "By every civilized and peaceful method we must strive for the rights which the world accords to men, clinging unwaveringly to those great words which the sons of the fathers would fain forget: 'We hold these truths to be self-evident: That all men are created equal.'" The design was likely created by DuBois himself, who was an admirer of Col. Shaw and mentions him in his writings.[23]

Later, DuBois was a founding member of the Niagara Movement, a precursor of the NAACP. The Niagara group held five annual meetings from 1905 through 1909 and used as its logo an outline sketch of the Shaw Memorial, depicting the colonel on horseback, his troops, and the hovering angel.[23]

Seal of the Niagara Movement, 1905-1910
From a woodcut. Courtesy Harper's Ferry National Historical Park,
National Park Service, Harper's Ferry, WV.

Reactions to the monument varied. Some observers were inspired to praise further the genuine heroism of Shaw and his men, while others contrasted the regiment's sacrifice for human and national values with the corruption or loss of some of these values in later decades. A former army chaplain, James M. Guthrie, for instance, urged "The visitor to Boston, Massachusetts who loves liberty and those who died for it, should not fail to see among its many shrines in that city, the monument erected to honor the memory of Colonel Robert Shaw (and his gallant regiment). . . . " He also contributed a special poetic tribute to the memory of Sergeant W. H. Carney entitled "The Old Flag Never Touched the Ground."

> March on, Black soldiers, in the van, free Negroes of the North,
> And each one prove yourself a man—a man of equal worth
> With any in the ranks of those who boast that they are White
> And for this reason are your foes: show them that you can fight.[24]

Of a very different tone was the sonnet "Robert Gould Shaw" by the leading Negro poet of his times, Paul Laurence Dunbar, who had in earlier, more optimistic days sung the praises of black troops in his ode to "The Colored Soldiers" which ended:

> And their deeds shall find record
> In the registry of Fame,
> For their blood has cleansed completely
> Every blot of Slavery's shame.

By 1900, however, Dunbar had become bitterly disillusioned. While his admiration for Shaw remained intense, he concluded in the poem "Robert Gould Shaw" that his sacrifice had been in vain, that the ideals for which he had died were no longer honored in the present.

> Why was it that the thunder voice of Fate
>   Should call thee, studious, from the classic groves,
>   Where calm-eyed Pallas with still footstep roves,
> And charge thee seek the turmoil of the state?
> What bade thee hear the voice and rise elate,
>   Leave home and kindred and thy spicy loaves,
>   To lead th' unfettered and despised droves
> To manhood's home thunder at the gate?
> Far better the slow blaze of Learning's light
>   The cool and quiet of her dearer fane,
> Than this hot terror of a hopeless fight
>   This cold endurance of the final pain—
> Since thou and those who died for right
>   Have died, the Present teaches, but in vain![25]

Yet another sort of interpretation was offered in 1900 by the poet William Vaughn Moody in "An Ode in Time of Hesitation" after seeing and reflecting upon the meaning of the monument. For him, the memorial inspired a sweeping condemnation of America's Philippine policy which stood in contradiction to the ideals expressed by Shaw and his men. Moody looked back on Shaw and the Fifty-Fourth as redeemers of our national purpose and honor. They followed the just and righteous path toward liberty where death and glory met

> To show all peoples that our shame is done,
> That once more we are clean and spirit-whole . . .

The validity of their sacrifice and our national honor, however, were again being put to the test by those who urged our country to subject yet other peoples—in the Pacific and in Cuba—this time to a colonial form of enslavement. Moody concluded with a challenge to our leadership to reject this course and to remain true to the ideals embodied in the Shaw monument.

> —O ye who lead,
> Take heed!
> Blindness we may forgive, but baseness we will smite.[26]

The American composer Charles Ives added another artistic dimension to the epic of Shaw and the Fifty-Fourth by juxtaposing music with poetry. His poem stands independently, preceding the score, rather than serving as a lyric; yet the images of both are coordinated to telling effect in their somber mood and plaintive tone. The underlying message of both is that of shared human purpose which Ives treats mournfully but with a sense of past and still-to-becontinued heroic resolve. First written about 1910, the piece was revised some twenty years later, and it was published in 1935 as "The Saint-Gaudens in Boston Common (Col. Shaw and his Colored Regiment)," the opening movement of his "orchestral set" *Three Places in New England.* The added dissonance of the new version undoubtedly added to its haunting air of mystery.[27]

The poem and the music are moving in their content and symbolism, as well as their emotional impact.

> Moving—Marching—Faces of Souls!
> Marked with generations of pain,
> Part-freers of a Destiny,
> Slowly, restlessly—swaying us on with you
> Toward other Freedom!
>
> ☾
>
> Above and beyond that compelling mass
> Rises the drum-beat of the common heart
> In the silence of a strange and
> Sounding afterglow
> Moving—Marching—Faces of Souls!

In the verses and the music Shaw and his phantom troops move ponderously and resolutely forward in their muffled march, shrouded in the darkness of death, relieved only by an afterglow of hope. They continue

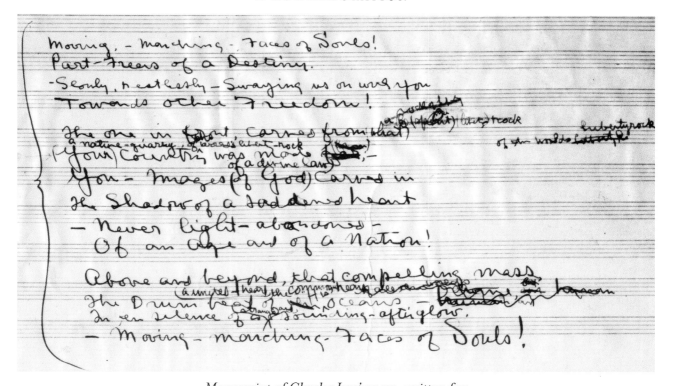

Manuscript of Charles Ives' poem, written for
"The Saint-Gaudens in Boston Common (Col. Shaw and His Colored Regiment)."
©1935 Merlon Music, Inc., Used by Permission of the Publisher. Image courtesy Yale University Library

the march toward other freedom and sway us to fall in beside them. The slow incessant drumbeat cadence of the march and of the common heart are one. It carries all forward beyond a fleeting crescendo of struggle, moving toward future fulfillment, as if following Saint-Gaudens's beckoning angel. The music and the poem end where they began, "Moving—Marching—Faces of Souls!"

If representations of Shaw and the Fifty-Fourth done in poetry, sculpture, oratory, music, and journalism were in large measure responsible for the continued march of the epic, the long-term underpinnings for its historiographical development came from Captain Luis Emilio's *History of the Fifty-Fourth Regiment of Massachusetts Volunteer Infantry, 1863-1865.* Although Emilio, as commander of Company E, had been an eyewitness and participant through much of the regiment's life, he based his regimental history additionally on an extensive compilation of contemporary letters, government reports, and journals as well as on conversations with other veterans of the unit. In 1890, the *History*'s publishers praised the work for being more than just another regimental history and one that would be of special interest to the new generation of the race from which the Fifty-Fourth was recruited. Its style was straightforward and its "plain narrative of the soldierly achievements of this black regiment is better evidence of the manly qualities of the race than volumes of rhetoric and panegyric could convey." They also thought it would appeal to the general public, for men of the regiment shared the patriotism and courage that characterized citizen soldiers in general. It was a typical regiment and yet it occupied a prominent position in representing the political policy of emancipation. The publishers felt fully justified in adding to the title the epithet, "A Brave Black Regiment." Later the Officers' Association of the Regiment adopted the work as its authorized history, and a second revised and corrected edition appeared in 1894. This work and other historical writings were to have an increasing impact on the epic-building process in its subsequent periods of revived development in the latter half of the twentieth century.

At mid-century, following decades of lapsed interest in Shaw and the Fifty-Fourth, two remarkably stark and beautiful poems, John Berryman's "Boston Common A Meditation upon the Hero" and Robert Lowell's "For the Union Dead (Relinquunt Omnia Servare Rem Publicam),"[27] served as a prelude to the epic's revival which followed in the years of the Civil War Centennial (1961-1965) and beyond. Both works draw inspiration from direct observation of the Saint-Gaudens monument and from reading the essay on it, on Shaw, and on the theme of civic courage by William James. Both poems, however, are written in dark tones reflecting a bitter disillusionment with the present, as if evoking the past in search of an elusive redemption. Both poets laud the past heroism of Shaw and his men but find their virtue anachronistic in face of the horrors of World War II and the cold detachment of contemporary society. For them the monument was less an "inciter" to continue the march or to pursue civic courage and more a symbol of an America gone by and now gone astray. If Moody had written ". . . in Time of Hesitation," Berryman and Lowell were writing seemingly in a time of anxiety and despair. The two poets were nonetheless inspired by the monument, moving from it to their social analysis, aesthetic expression, and musings of gloom.

"Boston Common" is the earlier, the longer, and the more cryptic of the two works. The poem centers on a visual and symbolic contrast between the heroic monument of the past and the "casual man" of the present, a dispossessed derelict who was sleeping beneath "the impressive genitals of the bronze charger."

Immortal heroes in a marble frame
Who broke their bodies on Fort Wagner's walls,
Robert Gould Shaw astride, and his
Negroes without name, who followed, who fell,
Screaming or calm, wet or cold, sick or oblivious.
Who now cares how? here they are in their prime,—

☾

Imperishable march below
The mounted man below the Angel, and
Under, the casual man, the possible hero . . .

The casual man lying passively "in shapeless failure" represented for Berryman "the last straw of contemporary thought." Now a "terrible shape, defeated and marvelous," the man under the stallion "is our whole hope . . . and our despair, the heart of the Future beating." He is in essence the statistical man of a non-caring society. Yet he may have been an unsung hero of forgotten "civic soul." Memorializing of heroes depended on "accidents of history." Honor should go to all who give, not to the selected few. For Berryman, the monument stands as a "frame of hope" and as a "dramatic bivouac" drawing attention to the unheeded casual man. Together in bronze and in life they stand to be reconciled in worship and in love. All of this is treated in a transcendent human sense, a recognition of the brotherhood of man, but the racial question is ignored. Had the derelict been black, the poem would have had an added message.[29]

Robert Lowell in "For the Union Dead" was still more pessimistic. While the "monument sticks like a fishbone in the city's throat," whatever message it may have had is ignored by a society in which "a savage servility slides by on grease." The poem is highly local in scope, a lament for the city of Boston, overwhelmed by the mechanized ugliness of the modern world, a world that itself seems much closer to disaster. He notes that there are no statues for World War II and refers to a photographic image of "Hiroshima boiling." The meaning of the Civil War seems to live on only in the Yankee stiffness of Shaw's personal image and in Lowell's nostalgia stripped of sentimentality. Saint-Gaudens's "Civil War relief" is now imperiled by the construction of a garage under Boston Common, where once "William James could almost hear the Bronze Negroes breath."

Its Colonel is as lean
as a compass-needle.

He has an angry wren-like vigilance,
a greyhound's gentle tautness,
he seems to wince at pleasure
and suffocate for privacy.

He is out of bounds now. He rejoices in man's lonely,
peculiar power to choose life and die—
when he leads his black soldiers to death,
he cannot bend his back.

On a thousand small town New England greens,
the old white churches hold their air
of sparse, sincere rebellion, frayed flags
quilt the graveyards of the Grand Army of the Republic

The stone statues of the abstract Union Soldier
grow slimmer and younger each year—
wasp-waisted, they doze over muskets
and muse through their sideburns . . .

Lowell's reverie remains focused on New England and on the Union. There is no sense of national reconciliation here, and the ideals of the past have yielded to the nightmares of the present As for race, he contrasts Colonel Shaw's "bell-checked Negro infantry" with the present-day "drained faces of Negro school-children . . ." rising "like balloons" on his television set.[30] Lowell, in fact, saw "For the Union Dead" as an "abolitionist poem" and later said, at the height of the civil rights struggle in 1964, that he lamented the loss of the old abolitionist spirit: "The terrible injustice, in the past and in the present, of the American treatment of the Negro is of the greatest urgency to me as a man and as a writer."[31] For Lowell, however, the monument seemingly embodied no hope, no living march, and no epic. It was a fading reminder of a dying past in the midst of a harsh, chaotic present increasingly bereft of traditional values. And yet, behind it all there was a glimmer of hope which stuck like a fishbone in the throat of the poet, provoking him to write one of his greatest works.

"For the Union Dead" later prompted American studies scholar Steven Axelrod to chart the poem's cultural pedigree.[32] For him, the poem expands upon the details of earlier works, and responds to their themes, and with it "Robert Lowell completes the task begun by James Russell Lowell, William

Vaughn Moody and John Berryman of transforming Shaw and the Fifty-Fourth Massachusetts from obscure Civil War heroes into national symbols, in order to dramatize an increasingly bleak moral situation." Writing in the early 1970s, Axelrod also refers briefly to the Saint-Gaudens's monument and to the William James dedication speech. Axelrod echoes Lowell's pessimism of a decade earlier in his contention that "These poets have been engaged in an extended losing battle with history," which has ended in moral defeat, leaving us only their artistic consolation."[33] While Axelrod was right in seeing the poems of Robert Lowell and his predecessors as part of a process, moving from local obscurity to national symbolism, he was mistaken in his conclusions. First, these poems were not in their own right sufficiently compelling or of broad enough appeal to complete the transformation to a national epic. Robert Lowell, however gifted a poet, was writing as yet another Bostonian and Harvard man—James Russell Lowell, Moody and Berryman were also all Harvard men—whose work added to the process of epic building but far from completed it. Second, Axelrod erred in seeing this as a completed process, which had ended with the closure of its moral significance. And third, he failed to grasp the overriding centrality of the Saint-Gaudens monument, which by its continued, commanding presence on the Boston Common stood as a beacon to steer the process through and well beyond the pessimism of Berryman, Lowell, and the period of the late 1960s and 1970s. Despite these shortcomings, Axelrod's article serves as one of the earliest and most important interpretations on the artistic continuity of the theme.

In the 1960s, however, the more positive and forward-looking continuations in the march of epic building came not in poetry but in other genres: history and biography. The Civil War Centennial and the most turbulent years of the civil rights movement coincided to spark an explosion of historical reassessments of the war in all of its complexities. In this, special attention was given to the role played by the African Americans in the war and their failure to achieve the full promise of equality in the decades that followed. The war, black history, and the symbolic sacrifice of Shaw and the Fifty-Fourth offered themes which were mutually supportive and which gradually became more central to a general discourse on America's past and present.

On the particular nexus of the war, blacks, and the Fifty-Fourth, no one has been more sustained and forceful in his contribution to academic history than Princeton's James M. McPherson. His pioneering work, *The*

Negro's Civil War, was first published in the same year of the Voting Rights Bill of 1965 and the close of the Centennial period. Quite contrary to the bleak prospects for humanity expressed earlier by Berryman and Lowell, the '60s were, as McPherson recalled when the book was reissued twenty five years later, ". . . a time of optimism in race relations much like the heady days of 1865, . . ." a time of looking forward to a bright future. Moreover, the demands of blacks for freedom and equality made in the 1960s were again as fresh and relevant as they had been a century earlier. Those were the days in which Americans were spellbound when President Lyndon Johnson echoed Martin Luther King's prophecy that, we shall overcome. The *Negro's Civil War* was the first book to express the war's history largely in the words of the blacks themselves, and the exploits of the Fifty-Fourth at Fort Wagner provided the principal focus of the chapter "Negro Soldiers Prove Themselves in Battle, 1863."[34] In the years following 1965, McPherson returned repeatedly to the theme of Shaw and his black regiment—in *Marching Toward Freedom: The Negro in the Civil War 1861-1867* (1967), in his "Foreword" to the reprint of Luis Emilio's *A Brave Regiment* (1969), in *Battle Cry of Freedom* (1988), in his "Foreword" to James Henry Gooding's letters, *On the Altar of Freedom* (1991).[35] Yet, despite his efforts and the ever-increasing flow of scholarship concerned with the African American experience in slavery and in the Civil War and its aftermath, McPherson admitted that there remained a general lack of awareness in the story of Shaw and the Fifty-Fourth until the public's interest was aroused by the film *Glory* in 1990. While raising questions in a review article, "The 'Glory' Story," about the conflict of historical accuracy and poetic or metaphoric truth, he stressed the potential of the film to reach millions of viewers, correcting earlier filmic distortions.[36]

Peter Burchard, previously most noted as an illustrator and writer of books for young people, made the greatest single contribution of the 1960s to the epic with his *One Gallant Rush: Robert Gould Shaw and His Brave Black Regiment.* Not only was this the first book-length biography of Shaw but it influenced subsequent writing on Shaw and his regiment both directly and through the film *Glory,* the screenplay of which was based largely on Burchard's book.[37] Burchard was first drawn to the theme while writing a piece for young readers on an earlier attack on Fort Wagner.[38] In *One Gallant Rush,* his interpretation is in the traditional vein of Shaw and the Fifty-Fourth as exemplars of the free black's ability to fight. Shaw had ultimately embraced the Negro's cause as his own personal crusade, and in dying with many of his men shared their heroic fate. The title is taken from Frederick Douglass' assessment of the Regiment's prospects: "The iron gate of our prison stands half open, one gallant rush . . . will fling it wide." Burchard ends the work with his own assessment of what Shaw meant to his compatriots:

> To New Englanders of his own time, Shaw, in his youthful Victorian innocence, seemed a kind of saint. In the last few months of his life, in his latter days and final hours, he had drawn on his forefathers' deep convictions and sense of duty and his own devotion to the cause which had rekindled the imaginations of New England's poets and scholars, preachers and teachers and practical men. In his last hours, Shaw had indeed caught fire and to those who had devoted their lives to the breaking of the back of the American shame, his death was an evening and a dawn.[39]

The centrality of the Saint-Gaudens memorial to the continuation of the epic was reaffirmed in a collaborative effort directed by Lincoln Kirstein, poet, cultural activist, publisher, and founder of the New York City Ballet, who had a long-standing interest in the contribution of blacks to the arts in America. Kirstein also felt a personal affinity with Colonel Shaw. He had, like Shaw, been raised in a civic-minded family in Boston and had roomed with a relation of Shaw's at Harvard. The project resulted in *Lay This Laurel: An Album on the Saint-Gaudens Memorial on Boston Common, Honoring Black and White Men Together Who Served the Union Cause with Robert Gould Shaw and Died with Him July 18, 1863* a striking book, rich in its blending of visual and verbal imagery, and beautifully produced by Kirstein's Eakins Press.[40]

Here, Richard Benson's poignant photographic study, comprising sixteen duo-tone plates of the monument, interspersed with epigraphs by Emily Dickinson, Frederick Douglass, Walt Whitman, and Abraham Lincoln, among others, is linked to Lincoln Kirstein's essay on the art of Saint-Gaudens and the historical events behind it. Their intent was to make the Shaw memorial available to "young Americans, patriots, art lovers, and others" beyond its fixed site in Boston, for it was a deserving "focus for pilgrimage, a civic shrine, a national reminder" and "an incomparable work of sculpture." This was art in service of patria and racial reconciliation. The critical times for black Americans in the 1960s and '70s called for a broader recognition of the work aesthetically and in its transcendent message. Kirstein further explained his intent:

It is especially to black artists—writers, composers, painters, sculptors, and choreographers—that this essay is aimed, for past any taint of racial chauvinism, Saint-Gaudens's work demonstrates how one vastly gifted, socially responsible white artist, operating on intractable material with an objective eye and resolute control over hand and eye, persisted through long years, resisting the easy impatience of his patrons, to achieve an individual representation worthy of the gigantic event the sculpture commemorates.

Of all of Saint-Gaudens's work, it is the monument to Robert Gould Shaw and his soldiers of the Fifty-Fourth Regiment of Massachusetts Volunteers which magnetizes the most passionate admiration and repays the closest attention.[41]

Kirstein's essay then traces the story of Shaw and of the Fifty-Fourth as well as that of the Saint-Gaudens monument. Not only does the work stress the role of the blacks and the joint nature of their sacrifice along with whites, but the book includes the first commemorative listing of the black enlisted men who fell at Fort Wagner.

Benson's photographs were done at a low point in the history of the monument's care and preservation ca. 1970. The figures are streaked with corrosion and the background matted with soot. Colonel Shaw's sabre is broken off within inches of the hilt, and even the stone frame is in ill-repair. Yet the power and message of the memorial are inescapable, and Kirstein concludes:

> Robert Shaw and his men march onward in the grave mutations of their modeling, moving towards some undefined, perhaps undefinable futurity in ominous ways less predictable than that which faced them when they went forth in the flesh more than a century ago.
>
> The exquisite justice of the placement of the mounted colonel whose leadership was as natural as breath itself, amidst the marching volunteers is on a level of translucent legibility and sudden reality unequaled in Western art. One may search many centuries in public places to discover a civic memorial so perfectly appropriate, achieved with such strength, subtlety, and finesse.[42]

A decade later in 1981 the civic consciousness of Boston was aroused to save the monument from possible collapse and destruction through the initiative of Boston's Friends of the Public Garden. Harvard's Fogg Museum made a study, funds were raised ($200,000), and restoration began. Through an article in *Time,* the "American Scene—In Boston Aid and Comfort for 'The Shaw'," Otto Friedrich brought the plight of the memorial to national attention. Henry Lee, president of the Friends of the Public Garden, whose great grandfather had been on the original Shaw Memorial committee, was one of the restoration project's prime movers. The monument was renewed and in a sense completed by the chiseled addition of the names of all of the black enlisted men who had fallen at Fort Wagner. David Mehegan noted in the *Boston Globe Magazine* that its restoration showed the almost magical way in which a work of art allied with stirring events and ideas can rally diverse people and move them to action. Henry Lee added, "The monument honors black and white men who served their common cause. Our hope was that in drawing attention to this, we could do a little bit toward healing some of our present conflicts." As for the future of "The Shaw," an endowment fund was also raised to assure its proper care and maintenance in perpetuity.[43] Thus restored and improved, the monument was ready for the mass distribution of its visual impact that would be provided by the film *Glory.*

In 1989 the release of the film *Glory* brought the epic of Shaw and the Fifty-Fourth to its fullest and most dramatic expression to date. In the film and subsequent video version the epic was to gain a mass national audience, spanning all geographic regions and all levels of culture from elite to popular, which had been left unreached by its earlier forms. In 1990 Ken Burns made television history, with his miniseries *Civil War,* which became the most highly acclaimed documentary ever produced. Thus the media of film and television worked in concert to raise popular interest in the Civil War to new heights and to capture the national imagination with the historical

Matthew Broderick as Col. Shaw.
Photo courtesy TriStar Films.

reality and symbolic significance of the sacrifice at Fort Wagner. The epic could now be widely seen as the embodiment of our prime and continuing values of unity, equality, and freedom.

Once an idea for a film has germinated, its realization is a collaborative affair from the outset. In most cases, as with *Glory,* it is impossible to give a preponderance of credit to one individual. The idea in this case came from Lincoln Kirstein, who had been committed to popularizing the epic of Shaw and particularly of his black soldiers since his Eakins Press project *Lay This Laurel.* It was this book, along with Peter Burchard's biography of Shaw, *One Gallant Rush*, and the letters of

Shaw himself, that served as the basis for the screenplay. Kirstein then kindled scriptwriter Kevin Jarre's interest in the project. Jarre in turn presented a draft script to Freddie Fields, who then became point man for the project and producer of the film. The early agreement of Matthew Broderick to play Shaw helped, and Field's success in drastically cutting cost projections, mainly through the use of non-professional battle "re-enactors," finally convinced Tri-Star's chairman Jeff Sagansky to undertake the making of *Glory*. Edward Zwick, another Harvard man with prior admiration for Shaw and the Fifty-Fourth, was chosen to direct and James Horner to compose the musical score. The film was generally well cast and many of its on-and off-screen par-

Denzel Washington as Trip.
Photo courtesy TriStar Films.

ticipants obviously felt a deep commitment to the film and to the underlying message of the epic which it dramatized.[44]

Like the Saint-Gaudens memorial, *Glory* is basically an ensemble piece presented on different levels of historical and metaphoric reality. At its core, the film is the story of the Fifty-Fourth Massachusetts Regiment. Its purpose, its formation, its training, its combat history through the gallant failure at Fort Wagner, and its transcendent message. It correctly describes the origin of the unit as the product of Boston's abolitionist fervor and portrays Colonel Shaw as its enabling agent. While Shaw serves both as the film's central character and as its narrator—by means of voiced-over excerpts from his wartime letters—he in no way overwhelms it. As in the monument, Shaw (played by Matthew Broderick) is treated in the equivalent of full round, not only as commander of the regiment but again as the only historically genuine personage in the film, aside from the minor figures of his family, Governor Andrew and Frederick Douglass.[45]

The four principal black characters—Trip (Denzel Washington), Rawlins (Morgan Freeman), Sharts (Jihmi Kennedy), and Searls (Andre Braugher)—are all fictional. They are highly individualized but are still

Morgan Freeman as Rawlins.
Photo courtesy TriStar Films.

types drawn to illustrate both the broad divergence of background of the soldiers and the wide range of attitudes they held concerning white and black society, the war, and the purpose of the Fifty-Fourth regiment. Their treatment in the film corresponds to the high relief used by Saint-Gaudens to depict the varying types he chose to represent with the bronze soldiers of his monument.

The ultimate level of metaphoric reality conveyed by the sculptor in his bas-relief angel is expressed in the film through James Horner's musical score which hovers just beyond the vision of the screen, as if urging the troops forward on their historic mission. Both the music and the angel serve as constant reminders to the viewer of this sense of yet-to-be-fulfilled mission which is central to their respective artistic formulations. Moreover, each representation was well suited to the audience of its day. Sculpted angels were as commonplace in the 1890s as stirring film scores in the 1990s. All three of the elements which were essentially linked to continue the march of the epic in Saint-Gaudens were thus recast, however inadvertently, in the film—Shaw, driven at first by duty and at the end by personal conviction; the black soldiers fighting for their manhood and national participation; and a divine expression of moral imperative—and again, as was the case in the monument, the closer to historical accuracy, the fuller the artistic representation.

In addition to fine acting and the compelling storyline, excellence in other elements behind the scenes—set design, costumes, sound, special effects, and especially the skilled direction of Edward Zwick—assured the superior quality of *Glory*'s production. Moreover, an unusually pervasive musical score by James Horner combined with *Glory*'s striking visual presentation, grounded in Freddi Francis's brilliantly realistic, sharp-focused color photography, to make an uncommonly strong impact in the viewer, demanding of him an emotional as well as intellectual response.

Throughout the film the motif of the march, musically and visually, is centrally geared to eliciting this response. Symbolic of order, discipline, training, mutual dependence, and dedication to mission the march motif builds from boot camp to parade leaving Boston, then from the regiment's first battle success in the woods of South Carolina to the initiation of the assault on Fort Wagner. The drumbeat cadence and whistle of the fifes draw the viewer forward along with the columns of marching black troops in their blue uniforms. The pace accelerates into quick time, and the soldiers follow Shaw and the flags of Massachusetts and the United States into battle. At the moment of Shaw's death, the full orchestra and the Boys' Choir of Harlem break into a Carmina-Burana-like exhortation which continues until the battle scene's abrupt conclusion.

At the conclusion of the film, following the brilliantly conceived and executed battle scenes of the climactic assault on Fort Wagner, the scene jumps to the mass burial of the Union dead where symbolically the bodies of Colonel Shaw and the rebellious Trip are thrown together into a common grave on the beach in front of the fort. The scene then shifts abruptly again to a full-frontal view of the Saint-Gaudens monument on Boston Common where Shaw and his men, no longer white and black, but immortalized in bronze, march on to a reprise of the score's march motif—at first heroic, and then plaintive—as a background against which are shown the film's initial credits. The rest of the crawl of credits is then seen against a black field while the musical score continues the march as if fading into the distance. Moreover, the musical handling of the entire march motif, rising to battle crescendo and then falling to reprise and fade out, is like an extended, more blatantly heroic, less dissonant, and demystified version of the Charles Ives, "Saint-Gaudens in Boston Common."[46] Thus, in its concluding moments, the film harkens back to the memorial as its final reference point, welding together the epic of Shaw and the Fifty-Fourth as history and art. The appearance of the monument serves a recapitulative gloss for the film just seen. The aesthetic and emotional impact of this is extraordinary.

Viewing it may encourage members of its audience to explore other versions of the epic, to read the long succession of poems from James Russell Lowell to Robert Lowell, to listen to Charles Ives' *Three Places in New England,* or to study the historical and biographical accounts written for adults or younger readers, or to see first hand, or in photographs, Saint-Gaudens's memorial with its undiminished power to inspire.

ENDNOTES

Epigraphs. Archibald MacLeish quoted in Daniel J Boorstin, *The Americans: The Democratic Experience* (New York: Random House, 1973), p 523. George H. Boker, "They buried him with his niggers'," in James M. Guthrie, *Camp-fires of the Afro-American or, The Colored Man as Patriot* (Cincinnati, Ohio: W.H. Ferguson, [1899?]), pp. 467-468.

1. [James Russell Lowell], "Memoriae, R.G.S., 1863," *Atlantic Monthly*, 13, no. 75 (January 1864), pp. 88-90.

2. Kevin Jarre, *Glory,* script rewrite by Eduard Zwick and Marshall Herskovitz (Los Angeles, CA: Glory Productions, 1988); originally issued as the film *Glory* ([Los Angeles] Tri-Star Productions, 1989); reissued on laser disc *Glory* ([Los Angeles] RCA, Columbia Pictures, Home Video, 1990).

3. William Wells Brown, *The Negro in the American Rebellion: His Heroism and His Fidelity.* (Boston, MA: Lee and Shepard, 1867; New York, NY: Johnson Reprint, 1968), pp. 157-158.

4. Ibid., pp 202-203.

5. *New York Times,* July 27, 1863, p. 1; *Harper's Weekly,* vol. 7, nos. 345, 346 (August 8, 15, 1863), pp. 509-510, 525-526; "The Gallant Charge of the Fifty-Fourth Massachusetts (Colored) Regiment," in *Currier and Ives, Chronicle of America*, edited by John Lowell Pratt (Maplewood, N.J.: Hammond, 1968), p. 165; Luis F. Emilio, *History of the Fifty-Fourth.* Regiment of Massachusetts Volunteer Infantry, 1863-1865, second edition, revised and corrected (Boston, MA:, Boston Book Company, 1897) reprinted as *A Brave Black Regiment,* with a foreword by James M. McPherson (New York, NY: Arno Press, 1969)

6. Brown, *The Negro in the American Rebellion,* pp. 210-211.

7. [James Russell Lowell], "Memoriæ Positum," pp. 88-90.

8. On Edmonia Lewis see Albert Boime, *The Art of Exclusion: Representing Blacks in the Nineteenth Century* (Washington, DC: Smithsonian Institution Press, 1990), pp. 161-171, which reproduces a photograph of her bust of Shaw; *The Booker T. Washington Papers* (Urbana, Ill: University of Illinois Press, 1975) vol.4, p 43, n.3.

9. Edward Atkinson, "History of the Shaw Monument by the Treasurer of the Fund," in *The Monument to Robert Gould Shaw, Its Inception, Completion, and Unveiling, 1865-1897* (Boston Houghton, Mifflin, and Company, 1897), pp. 7-13, and "The Shaw Memorial and the Sculptor St. Gaudens, I. The History of the Monument," *Century Magazine,* vol. 54, no. 2 (June 1897), pp 176-178; Burke Wilkinson, *Uncommon Clay: The Life and Works of Augustus Saint-Gaudens,* (New York, NY: Harcourt, Brace, Jovanovich, 1985), pp. 279-288, The Reminiscences of Augustus Saint-Gaudens, edited by Homer Saint-Gaudens (New York, NY: The Century Company, 1913), vol. 2, pp. 78-84.

10. An early description and evaluation of the monument is William A. Coffin, "The Shaw Memorial and the Sculptor St. Gaudens, 11. The Sculptor St. Gaudens. "*Century Magazine,* vol. 54, no. 2 (June 1897), pp. 179-193. For recent treatments see Wilkinson, *Uncommon Clay, pp. 274-288;* Louise Hall Tharp, Saint Gaudens and the Gilded Era (Boston: Little, Brown and Company, 1969), pp. 267-283; Boime, *Art of Exclusion,* pp. 199-219. Boime's interpretation is especially interesting as it rests largely on a discussion of the work of a nineteenth-century black art historian, Freeman Henry Morris Murray, *Emancipation and the Freed in American Sculpture: A Study in Interpretation* (Washington, DC: the author, 1916).

11. Brooklyn Museum, *The American Renaissance, 1876-1917* (New York, NY: Pantheon Books, 1979).

12. Coffin, "The Sculptor St. Gaudens," p. 184.

13. Lorado Taft, *The History of American Sculpture* (New York, NY: Macmillan, 1903), pp. 302-304, 363, as quoted in Boime, *Art of Exclusion,* pp. 204-205.

14. Quoted in Boime, *Art of Exclusion, p. 204.* Boime concludes that Murray's personal attachment to the Shaw monument led him to see it as "the ideal memorial, an excellent work of art with the correct' ideological message." Boime has strong reservations about this because of what he contends was Saint Gaudens's underlying racism, pp. 199-219.

15. Wilkinson, *Uncommon Clay, p. 274.*

16. Ibid., p. 286, "Unveiling the Shaw Monument, May 31, 1897," *in The Monument to Robert Gould,* pp 37-49.

17. Boston. Evening Transcript, June 1, 1897 quoted in *The Booker T. Washington Papers,* vol. 1, pp 109-112. See also "Ceremonies at the Music Hall," in *The Monument to Robert Gould Shaw,* pp. 52-96.

18. *The Booker T. Washington Papers,* vol. 4, pp. 264, 270-272, 285, 292, 295, letters exchanged between Washington and William James regarding their Shaw Memorial addresses.

19. Ibid., vol. 1, pp. 106- 109, vol. 4, pp. 300-302.

20. William James, "Robert Gould Shaw," in *Memories and Studies* (New York Longman's Green, and Co., 1917), pp 40-61. His description of Shaw as a "blue-eyed child of fortune." (p. 40) may have been slightly incorrect. The copy of The *Monument to Robert Gould Shaw* owned by the University of California Davis Library had originally been presented to Mrs. Francis G. Shaw, Robert's mother. Among the handwritten corrections in this copy, one appearing in the address given by Major Henry Lee Higginson corrects his text which refers to Shaw's "merry *blue* eyes" to "light hazel."

21. Henry Lee Higginson, "Address," in *The Monument to Robert Gould Shaw,* pp. 21,36.

22. W.E.B. DuBois, "Strivings of the Negro People," *Atlantic Monthly,* 80, no. 478 (August 1897), pp. 194-198; *The Souls of Black Folk* (New York: Penguin Books, 1989), pp. 43-45, 50

23. The logo is on exhibition by the National Park Service at Harper's Ferry National Monument. On DuBois and the Niagara Movement, see David Levering Lewis, W.E.B. DuBois: *Biography of a Race, 1868-1919* (New York: Henry Holt, 1993), pp.315-342
Dr. Lewis has found little information on the origin of the seal, but believes DuBois, who considered himself a graphic artist, most likely

designed the logo. DuBois greatly admired Shaw and the 54th Regiment. Telephone interview, March 2002

24. James M. Guthrie, *Campfires of the Afro-American,* pp. 468-473.

25. *The Collected Poetry of Paul Laurence Dunbar,* ed. by Joan M. Brixton (Charlottesville University of Virginia Press, [1993]), pp. 50-52, 221.

26. William Vaughn Moody, "An Ode in Time of Hesitation," *Atlantic Monthly,* vol. 85, no. 511 (May 1900), pp. 593-598.

27. Charles E. Ives, *Three Places in New England* (Boston: C.C. Birchard, 1935); *Charles Ives— Memos,* edited by John Kirkpatrick (New York: W.W. Norton 1972), pp. 85-87. Elliot Carter in *Charles Ives Remembered. An Oral History,* edited by Vivian Perlis (New Haven Yale University Press, 1974), p. 138. For a recorded version, consult Howard Hanson conducting the Eastman-Rochester Orchestra, Charles Ives, *Three Places in New England* (New York, NY: Polygram "Mercury" Records).

28. John Berryman, "Boston Common: A Meditation upon a Hero," in *The Dispossessed* (New York: William Sloan Associates, 1948), pp. 63-68, Robert Lowell, "For the Union Dead, Relinquunt Omnia Servare Rem Publicam,"' in *Life Studies and For the Union Dead* (New York, NY: Farrar, Straus, and Giroux, 1964), pp. 70-72.

29. Berryman, "Boston Common," pp. 63-68.

30. Lowell, "For the Union Dead," pp. 70-72.

31. Robert Lowell as quoted in lan Hamilton, *Robert Lowell: A Biography (New* York: Random House, 1982), p. 281.

32. Steven Axelrod, "Colonel Shaw in American Poetry: For the Union Dead and its Precursors," *American Quarterly,* vol. 24, no. 4 (October 1972), pp. 523-537.

33. Ibid., pp. 523, 530-531, 537.

34. James M. McPherson, *The Negro's Civil War: How American Blacks Felt and Acted During the War for the Union* (New York, NY: Ballantine Books 1991; first published New York Pantheon Books, 1965), pp xi-xvi I, 191-196.

35. James M. McPherson, *Marching Toward Freedom: The Negro in the Civil War, 1861-1867* (New York: Alfred A. Knopf, 1967), "Foreword" in Luis Emilio, *Brave Black Regiment, Battle Cry of Freedom: The Civil War Era* (New York, NY:

Oxford University Press, 1988); and "Foreword" in Gooding, *On the Altar of Freedom.*

36. McPherson, *The Negro's Civil War,* pp. xii-xiii, James M. McPherson, "The *Glory* Story," *New Republic,* vol. 202 (January 8, 15, 1990), pp. 22-23, 26-27.

37. Peter Burchard, *One Gallant Rush: Robert Gould Shaw and His Brave Black Regiment* (New York St. Martins, 1965) The paperback edition, issued in 1989, has added to the cover: *Glory . . . The True Historical Saga,* Dramatized in the Major Motion Picture *Glory.*

38. Peter Burchard, telephone conversation, December 3, 1993.

39. Burchard, One Gallant Rush, pp. xii, 147.

40. Richard Benson and Lincoln Kirstein, *Lay This Laurel: an Album on the Saint-Gaudens Memorial on Boston Common: Honoring Black and White Men Together Who Served the Union Cause with Robert Gould Shaw and Died with Him July 18, 1863* (New York: Eakins Press, 1973), unpaged, see "Acknowledgments" at end, telephone conversation with Leslie Katz, editor of the project for the Eakins Press, December 9, 1993. In a recent study Nicholas Fox Weber treats Kirstein as one of our cultural patron saints in *Patron Saints: Five Rebels Who Opened America to a New Art, 1928-1934* (New York, NY: Knopf, 1992).

41. Ibid., unpaged, see the first two pages of Kirstein's essay.

42. Ibid., unpaged, see the Benson photographs and the last and the 95th to the last pages of the Kirstein essay.

43. Otto Friedrich, "American Scene—In Boston: Aid and Comfort for 'The Shaw'," *Time,* vol. 117, no. 14 (April 6, 1981), pp. 4-5; David Mehegan, "For These Union Dead," *Boston Globe Magazine* (September 5, 1982), pp. 10-11, 29, 32-33.

44. Benson and Kirstein, *Lay This Laurel,* and Burchard, *One Gallant Rush.* The sequence of involvement in the project comes from telephone conversations with Burchard, December 3, 1993; Leslie Katz, December 9, 1993; Edward Zwick, January 5, 1994; Freddie Fields, March 9, 1994.

45. Jarre, *Glory* [script], *Glory* [film]; *Glory* [laser disc].

46. Ives, *Three Places in New England*

Dismantling of the Shaw Memorial,
August 1996 by Daedalus, Inc.

CONSERVATION OF THE SHAW MEMORIAL

by Brigid Sullivan

The conservation history of the plaster cast of the *Shaw Memorial* spans almost exactly one century, dating from the first major conservation campaign in 1901 when the plaster, upon return from exhibition in Paris, was prepared for exhibit at the Pan-American Exposition in Buffalo, to the conservation effort to prepare it for exhibit in the National Gallery of Art in Washington, D.C. This recent effort was initially born of a growing concern over the physical deterioration of the Shaw by years of exposure to ambient conditions in its outdoor exhibit location at Saint-Gaudens National Historic Site in Cornish, New Hampshire. Though providing shelter from direct rain and snow, the three-sided roofed structure in which the Shaw was displayed provided no protection against damaging extremes of both temperature and relative humidity, nor against abrasive and corrosive airborne particles and gaseous pollutants destructive to the plaster over time.

CONDITION

Decorative Surface:

Various campaigns of localized surface treatments and cosmetic interventions over the years resulted in a distractingly patchy overall appearance.

When the surface of the Shaw was examined by conservators from the National Park Service and from Daedalus, Inc. shortly before the conservation project began, flaking of the metal leaf coating was apparent in several areas on the front, most notably on the proper right trouser cuff of the drummer, and the side and bottom of the drum. Small blisters and fissures were visible throughout the surface.

Plaster:

Numerous small surface cracks and superficial chips were observed and recorded before the plaster was dismantled. Stress cracks were pronounced along the front of the base in four locations, and across the rear legs and the right front leg of the horse.

In general, when the sculpture was dismantled, the plaster was found to be in stable condition. The past conservation campaigns, which included consolidation of the surface (with Acryloid B-72) and gilding with metal composition leaf followed by toning layers and protective coatings of lacquer and wax, served to protect the plaster from exposure to the elements. However, when disassembly began, the plaster in some areas such as the upper background section containing the angel relief, were found to be friable and porous.

Background relief section showing fill (textured) along damaged join line.

Dismantling and removal of overfill along the section joins revealed extensive previous repair to damaged edges of the sections and many layers of overfill that had been applied to disguise misalignments in previous installations.

96

Armature:

Of greatest concern was the deteriorated condition of the interior armature support. The 1992 Condition Report, prepared by the Center for Conservation and Technical Studies noted visible rust on exposed areas of the iron wire armature elements on Shaw's spur and on the horse's tail, mane, reins, bridle and bit, on the front of the sculpture. In the back, rusting of exposed iron and staining of plaster indicated active corrosion. The increase in volume of the armature due to corrosion, had caused chipping, cracking and detachment of plaster both in contact with, and adjacent to, rusting iron elements. Some of the exposed thinner wire elements had broken.

The Shaw was again examined in 1995 by Conservator Clifford Craine of Daedalus, Inc. who noted that in some places the exposed wood elements of the armature structure were soft and spongy with rot. In many areas, the wood was no longer in direct contact with the plaster, because of the displacement of the plaster in response to expansion and contraction of the wood and fiber with changes in relative humidity and temperature.

Mr. Craine's assessment of the overall stability of the sculpture at the time of his examination was as follows:

> The actual present condition of the sculpture is in reality difficult to ascertain with any degree of certainty. This is because the front of the cast is covered with a restored decorative surface, and the back of the cast is covered by the added external armature, and a concrete wall. However, the presence of many small cracks in the surface of the sculpture was noted as early as the 1981 Fogg conservation treatment record, and again in the 1989 Dennis and Craine memo. Pronounced cracking was noted along some of the seams, especially in the upper right hand corner and on the horizontal surfaces of the base. Losses of plaster surface adjacent to rusting wire armatures in the horse's mane and elsewhere have also required on-going conservation treatment. *These observations, coupled with the finding that many of the components of the 1959 external armature are not well adhered, suggest that the structural stability of the sculpture in its present environment and its present configuration is questionable. It seems prudent to assume that if conditions are unchanged, deterioration will only continue.*[1]

In pursuit of long-range preservation of this unique and important work of art, the project to make a mold and replicate the plaster in bronze for continued display on-site, was inaugurated in 1996 by the Trustees of the Saint-Gaudens Memorial and the National Park Service. Arrangements were made to loan the original plaster cast to the National Gallery of Art in

Washington D.C. where it would be safely exhibited and enjoyed by thousands of visitors.

Understanding the condition of the Shaw Memorial in the context of its complex treatment history was necessary to develop an appropriate conservation approach for all phases of the project: disassembly, moldmaking, reassembly, and final surface treatment. Clifford Craine of Daedalus Art Conservation Inc., Cambridge, MA, was contracted by the National Park Service and the National Gallery of Art as the project chief conservator for all phases, including reassembly and surface treatment at the National Gallery in Washington, D.C. Mr. Craine had previous first-hand experience with the Shaw Memorial when he worked on the last major conservation campaign in the early 1980s as a staff member of the Center for Conservation and Technical Studies.

Pavilion for the Shaw Memorial, 1959-1996.
Saint-Gaudens NHS, Cornish, NH

Conservation History:

The plaster cast was executed by Saint-Gaudens in his New York studio at about the same time that the bronze cast of the Memorial was being completed for installation on the Boston Common in 1897 (fragments of an 1896 newspaper were embedded in the plaster). He intended the plaster cast to be shown along with other examples of his work, at various exhibit venues. The plaster Shaw version differs from the bronze, primarily in the detail of the background bas-relief angel, which Saint-Gaudens continued to develop artistically until 1900. The plaster version was intended for exhibit, specifically at the 1898 Paris Salon *Societe Nationale des Beaux Arts* to be followed by exhibit in the 1900 *Exposition Universelle* in Paris, and finally, the 1901 *Pan American Exposition in Buffalo*. The design of the sculpture in about twenty-one sectional units allowed it to be broken down for shipment and reassembled in various exhibit venues. Each move, however, required installing support armature in the back, filling and finishing of section joins as well as an overall final surface treatment to achieve the appearance of a solid sculptural unit.

Installation at the National Gallery marked the ninth episode of complete dismantling and reassembly of the plaster cast in its history, and the tenth episode of complete surface treatment. The recent effort developed a surface treatment plan consistent with the last appearance personally directed and endorsed by Saint-Gaudens, as substantiated by archival documentation, and physical evidence obtained by scientific examination.

SURFACE TREATMENT HISTORY: DOCUMENTARY EVIDENCE
Treatment as Directed by Saint-Gaudens:

In January 1898, the plaster cast was packed at the New York studio by art packers from the Boston Museum of Fine Arts and shipped to Paris. The cast was initially reassembled at Saint-Gaudens' Paris Studio in April, then dismantled again and transported to the site of the 1898 Salon.[2] We presume that Saint-Gaudens directed reassembly and cosmetic finishing of the Memorial, but little is known of the surface treatment or appearance other than that which can be extrapolated from inspection of a photogravure image showing the Memorial on display at the Salon.

When the Memorial was next moved in 1900 to the Grand Palais for the *Exposition Universelle*, it is clear that Saint-Gaudens was actively involved in the surface treatment of the reassembled plaster. William A. Coffin, Artistic Director of American Art for the Exposition, wrote that 'The Shaw had been colored. It was all set up and it was 'finished,' but Saint-Gaudens told me that it was too dark and he was having it all done over with a tint and rub-down to make it lighter."[3] ". . . he is having the Shaw colored bronze. . . ."[4]

In 1901, the *Shaw Memorial* was shipped to Buffalo, New York for exhibit in the Pan American Exposition. Documentation in the William A. Coffin papers, notes that "after Henry (Hering) had finished setting it up, the color was matched on the joints and repaired places as closely as possible" indicates that the surface appearance was unchanged from the Paris Exposition.[5] In fact, a photograph of the opening day of the Pan American Exposition Fine Arts Building shows the *Shaw Memorial* as yet unfinished with section join lines clearly visible.

In March 1905, the cast was to be exhibited at the Inaugural Exhibition of the Buffalo Fine Arts Academy, also known as the Albright Art Gallery, requiring a renewed surface treatment. The process of gold-leaf gilding was interrupted on March 15 when the Shaw was dismantled and moved to a different location within the gallery. The Albright Art Gallery Architect Edward B. Green wrote to Saint-Gaudens in 1905 that "The flying figure on the Shaw Memorial has been partly covered with gold leaf . . . we stopped the work because the Fine Arts Academy has decided to change the position of the Memorial, and therefore, it must be taken down and moved."[6]

The plaster was exhibited at the Albright Art Gallery at the end of May, although a final surface treatment was not undertaken until July by James Earl Fraser who came to Buffalo as directed by Saint-Gaudens to "clean, paint and bronze" the Shaw. This might be interpreted as darkening the bright gold leaf by toning layers.[7]

The Shaw Memorial remained on exhibit in the gallery until 1919, at which time it was removed from view by the simple expedient of constructing a new gallery wall in front of it, rather than removing it from the building altogether. It remained out of view for thirty years until 1949, when it was finally dismantled and moved as part of a major gallery renovation of the museum, now known as the Albright-Knox Gallery. Interestingly, the contractor hired to oversee the disassembly was Mr. Joseph Balk, who, as a young man, helped dismantle the Shaw at the close of the Inaugural Exhibit in Buffalo in 1901. The plaster was shipped in sections to Cornish, New Hampshire where it remained in storage until 1959, when the decision was made to exhibit it on the grounds of Saint-Gaudens home and studio under the sponsorship of the Saint-Gaudens Memorial.

Surface Treatment after Saint-Gaudens's Lifetime:

In 1959, the Saint-Gaudens Memorial Trustees contracted New York sculptor John Terken, to install and cosmetically repair the Memorial for exhibit. Ten years later, Terken described this project in a letter written to the Saint-Gaudens National Historic Site, "the original (gold) leaf had sustained much damage and would have been prohibitive to restore. Consequently, I painted it with flat oil paint, first dark, then light. This was followed by varnish and gold powder in stipple effect." In 1962, as reported in the Claremont (N.H.) *Daily Eagle,* Terken was again contracted to undertake a full restoration of the Memorial because "Three years of exposure to temperature change and considerable moisture at the Cornish site had resulted in chipping and flaking of the plaster from which the cast is constructed and a general undermining of the material itself was feared." The restoration consisted of "sealing of exposed plaster sections and the addition of a 'patina'; a gray-green coloring to resemble weathered bronze, and gilding to add highlights."[8]

In 1981, the National Park Service embarked on a major conservation campaign to stabilize and restore the Shaw to its original appearance. Nearly twenty years of weathering, and application of maintenance coats of paint since the Terken restoration had resulted in an unattractive chalky appearance. The Center for Conservation and Technical Studies at the Fogg Museum, was contracted to undertake the conservation, and, in 1981, did scientific analysis of the existing layers of surface coatings prior to treatment. In 1982–83, the thick disfiguring paint layers were removed, and the surface regilded with synthetic gold-size, and composition leaf (faux gold leaf) toned with Liquitex emulsion glazes.

In 1986, the Center for Conservation and Technical Studies again treated the plaster to correct discoloration caused by combined effects of weathering, accumulated dirt and pollen. The Shaw was cleaned, reglazed, and inpainted with Liquitex emulsion paint to integrate overly bright areas. From 1986 to 1990, minor structural repairs such as filling plaster losses, consolidating flaking paint, and reattaching recovered loose fragments, were done by the Center for Conservation and Technical Studies, but most of the conservation work prior to the recent project was cosmetic in nature.

Surface Treatment: Scientific Examination

Because some plaster rifles, the painted wood sword, and painted metal sword hilt, are detachable pieces, and those elements were missing in the Boston monument, they were used in 1981 for replication during restoration of the Shaw Memorial in Boston. When these pieces were stripped with solvent in preparation for molding, the conservators noted that the following sequence of layers were revealed in the stripping process from the outermost layer, or last surface treatment, to the plaster substrate:

> Green paint
> Turquoise paint

Darkened or tinted resin
Metal paint (bronze? gold?)
Green paint
Plaster – wood – metal

It is interesting to compare this observation with microanalytical research findings carried out at the same time by the Center, and subsequently by both the Boston Museum of Fine Arts and the National Gallery of Art.

1981 Analytical Research by the Center for Conservation and Technical Studies

In 1981, the Center for Conservation and Technical Studies examined six cross sections of surface samples by reflected light microscopy, and one sample was analyzed by scanning electron microscopy with an attached x-ray spectrometer to determine the elements present in the various layers. Pigments in the lower levels were also examined by polarized microscopy.

At least nine distinct layers were identified in all samples, starting with three initial layers common to all: a first layer containing white pigments with chrome yellow and charcoal black which would create a drab olive green color, a second lighter layer also containing synthetic ultramarine blue, creating a pale green, and finally, a third layer with blue, yellow and black, with less white, creating a darker green appearance. Subsequent layers were identified as varnish layers and yellow ground, or mordant layers for metal leaf, with an additional medium-rich dark green layer in which metal leaf, identified as gold with occasional brass leaf identified in layer six and beyond.

The layers associated with the metal leafing (4-6), as well as the lowermost three paint layers were found to be continuous, indicating that the lower layers were in good condition when the metal leaf was applied.

1997 Analytical Research by the Museum of Fine Arts, Boston

With the goal of comparing cross-section layer sequences identified by microscopy to the documentary records describing treatment campaigns, additional analyses were conducted in 1997 by the Research Department of the Boston Museum of Fine Arts. Nine samples were selected from locations likely to contain an uninterrupted surface layer sequence predating the conservation campaign of 1983. At that time the Memorial was largely stripped of easily removable layers, and the surface regilded with brass leaf and toned.

The samples were examined by reflected light and ultraviolet florescence microscopy. Most of the samples were also analyzed by x-ray florescence in an electron beam microprobe, for general identification of pigments and composition of leaf layers. Isolated layers from selected samples were also analyzed by FTIR microscopy for pigment identification, and by GS/MS for specific medium identification.

The MFA analysis identified six layers common to all samples in sequence from the initial green paint layers directly on the plaster (layers 1 through 3); to a layer of untinted medium (layer 4) which may be a layer of tonal adjustment to the underlying green paint; followed by a layer (layer 5) which appears to be a common ground or mordant for the metal leaf (layer 6).

Many additional layers were found in most of the samples, but no direct evidence of toning layers was seen as a common layer. It is possible that toning may have been done by thin pigmented varnish or shellac glazes, or even by tinted wax, which might not have been durable enough to withstand abrasion by years of cleaning and preparation for new surface treatments. The written research report submitted by the MFA, states that organic colorants may have been used that would not have been readily detectable by the analytical methods used in this research.

1997 Analytical Research by the National Gallery of Art, Washington, D.C.

In 1997, a cross-section of a sample taken from the background angel figure before the surface was prepared for molding. It was mounted and analyzed by the National Gallery of Art, and shows the full stratigraphy of the Shaw coatings. In the stratigraphic sequence, the latest conservation campaigns from 1983 to 1992, are represented by approximately nine or ten layers that contain combinations of bronze leaf, metallic bronze powder, and dark reddish-brown layers. The restoration campaign of 1959-1962, when the Memorial was installed in Cornish and painted green, is also clearly represented in about six layers, starting with a thick plaster layer probably dating to the reassembly in Cornish by Mr. Terken, and subsequent layers of greenish blue paint. Beneath this the 1905 surface treatment for exhibition at the Inaugural Exposition of the Buffalo Fine Arts Academy is suggested by distinct layers of bole (yellow medium rich layer) and metallic gold leaf, and is consistent with archival evidence. A green layer directly above the plaster corroborates analyses by the MFA and the Center for Conservation and Technical Studies, and evidence of metal leaf or powder in a coat directly above the green paint may suggest the "tint and a rub-down to make it lighter" as described by William A. Coffin in Paris in 1900.[9]

The NGA also conducted SEM/EDS analyses of an additional six samples taken from areas least likely to have been disturbed by conservation campaigns before 1983. This was an attempt to gather more information about layer sequence and composition that could be useful in determining the correct historic appearance of the Shaw to guide conservation efforts.

From the plaster substrate outward, the following common layers were identified. These layers are not always in the actual numerical order of sequential layers identified in each sample, but are numbered here in order to represent shared features among samples.

Representative of the Paris Exhibitions of 1898 and 1900:

1. Thin grayish green (6 samples)
2. Light blue (6 samples)
3. Bluish green (5 samples)

Representative of The Interrupted Campaign of Gilding at The Albright Gallery Exhibition in 1905:

4. Clear coating or size (5 samples)
5. Bright yellow (lead chromate, mordant for leafing) (4 samples)
6. Associated metal layers : gold (3 samples); brass (1 sample)
7. Clear green (3 samples)
8. Bright yellow (mordant for leafing) (3 samples)
9. Associated metal layers: gold (2 samples); brass (1 sample)
   (A discontinuous layer of toned coating or size appears above this layer on 1 sample)

Representative of the Terken Restoration in 1959-62:

10. Whitish layer (4 samples)
    (Traces of dirt and grime follow on one sample. The green paint used by Terken was probably removed in the 1982 restoration)

Representative of the Fogg Restoration of 1982:

11. Clear coating of size (5 samples)
12. Brass metal leaf (5 samples)
13. Remnants of dark brownish layer of earths and blacks (5 samples)
14. Coating or size (2 samples)

It is interesting to see that both the MFA and the NGA analyses identify the concurrent use of gold and brass leaf. Sculptural works contemporary to the Shaw, such as the Amor Caritas and the Victory figure of the magnificent Sherman Monument and the, demonstrate the artist's use of gilding bronze surfaces to enhance his artistic vision. He was clearly working with this technique in 1905 at the time of the plaster Shaw's exhibition at the Albright Gallery in Buffalo. In pursuit of achieving the aesthetic appearance of his gilded bronzes, Saint-Gaudens may have used a combination of the metal leaf available to him to create a gilded surface, over which toning layers could enhance the sculptural quality of the work. Evidence of toning layers over metal leaf appear only sporadically, if at all, in the six sample layer sequences, but do appear in the layer sequence of the two samples taken by the NGA before the disassembly and preparation for molding.

Based on the array of analyses conducted by the technical laboratories for the National Park Service and the National Gallery of Art, a determination was made in May, 1997, to seek a base coating patination that would closely recall the gold leaf with overglazes of umber and translucent green hues. This replicated as closely as possible the final treatment of the cast done during the sculptor's lifetime.

DISASSEMBLY

When the Shaw Memorial was taken apart for shipment to Cornish in 1949, contemporary newspaper coverage stated that the memorial was composed of "21 pieces that make up the work of art."[10] In 1992, The Center for Conservation and Technical Studies examined the Shaw, and identified eighteen component sections from evidence of join lines visible on the surface of the sculpture. Joins in the surrounding cornice and side columns make up the rest of the component sections. During the Terken restoration, the plaster sculpture was installed within a three-sided, roofed structure with a cement block back wall. The relief was anchored by means of twisted metal wires held by metal clips set into the mortar between the concrete blocks. No record was made of the number and exact location of the attachments, and visible access to the back of the sculpture was extremely limited due to the proximity of the wall.

In preparation for disassembly, a radiographic examination of the Shaw was made by Conam Inspection Services of Auburn, MA using a radiation source and Structurix x-ray film from Agfa Division of Bayer

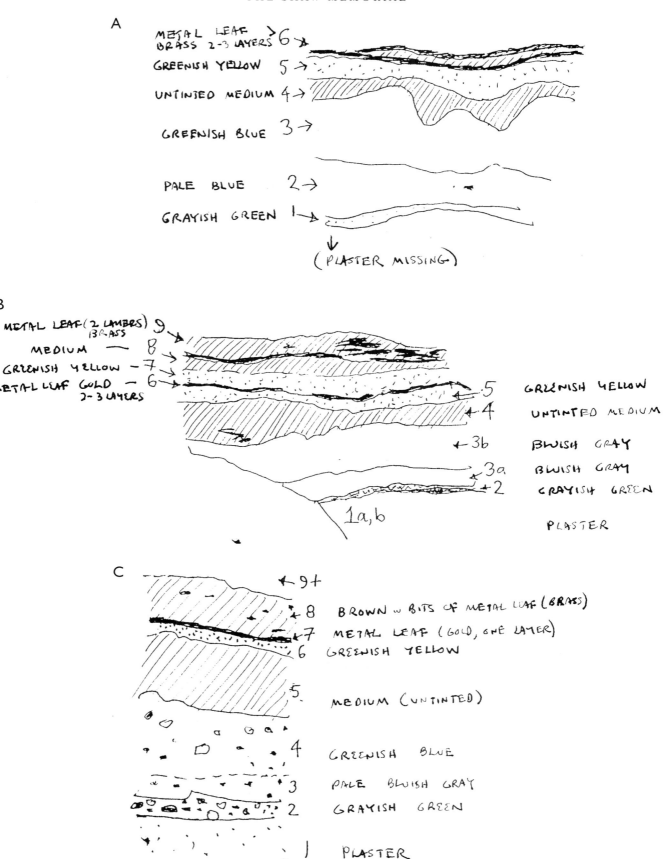

A

METAL LEAF
BRASS 2-3 LAYERS 6 →
GREENISH YELLOW 5 →
UNTINTED MEDIUM 4 →

GREENISH BLUE 3 →

PALE BLUE 2 →
GRAYISH GREEN 1 →

↓
(PLASTER MISSING)

B

METAL LEAF (2 LAYERS) 9 →
13 BRASS
MEDIUM — 8 →
GREENISH YELLOW — 7 →
METAL LEAF GOLD — 6 →
2-3 LAYERS

5 → GREENISH YELLOW
4 → UNTINTED MEDIUM

3b → BLUISH GRAY

3a → BLUISH GRAY
2 → GRAYISH GREEN

1a,b

PLASTER

C

9+ →
8 → BROWN w BITS OF METAL LEAF (BRASS)
7 → METAL LEAF (GOLD, ONE LAYER)
6 GREENISH YELLOW

5 MEDIUM (UNTINTED)

4 GREENISH BLUE

3 PALE BLUISH GRAY
2 GRAYISH GREEN

1 PLASTER

A, B, and C. Samples taken from: (A) horse's back leg near rump; (B) back-most soldier's head by ear; and (C) soldier group directly behind horse, behind ear of first soldier.

Corporation. The examination, directed by Clifford Craine, was made to identify the location of original Roman joins, internal armature and method of attachment to the rear wall so an appropriate disassembly strategy could be developed.

Approximately twenty-four exposures were made, mostly by inserting the sheets of film between the plaster cast and the inside of the concrete wall. The radiographs showed that although the Balk diagram was essentially accurate, many of the original joints in the plaster had been destroyed and/or modified by subsequent campaigns of installation and disassembly. In most instances, pipe was inserted through both ends of the original roman joins, and plastered in place. The original joints of the horse's legs and neck were bridged internally with burlap and pipe, making the horse a single unit. The figure of Shaw was also modified, permanently attaching his proper right leg to his body by means of a pipe through the original roman join. The radiographs also showed that additional iron pipe was used to support the exterior of some of the cast sections at the back of the relief, and also used to attach individual sections together. It was clear from this examination that it would not be possible to dismantle the Shaw in its original component parts.

In addition, a series of misalignments in the back sections containing the angel relief, resulted in a distortion of the cornice line, most noticeable at the egg and dart molding band. These sections were reinforced with metal pipe in the 1959 installation, and because of the thinness of

Diagram of Shaw's component sections by Joseph Balk, 1949.

the plaster in the upper backgound area, the mis-alignment cannot now be safely corrected in the original plaster.

The horse was also incorrectly placed, and tilted forward at an unnatural angle, but because the horse section can be removed from the surrounding sculpture, this feature was corrected when the cast was reassembled.

The Shaw was dismantled by Daedalus, Inc. in a six-week period in August and September, 1996. The back concrete block wall was dismantled in stages from top to bottom and side to side, as the disassembly of the sculpture progressed.

During the disassembly, the extent of the damage and material loss of section edges through previous installations, was found to be significant, especially in the base, with extensive overfill of adjoining sections. The fill material between sections was removed with chisels and scalpels. Each section was secured with webbing and lifted by means of a block and tackle to a prepared staging area for crating. The sections were moved by Fine Arts Express to the Daedalus conservation laboratory in Boston for conservation and preparation for mold-making.

Preparation for Mold-Making

At the Daedalus studio in Boston, the 1959 external armature elements were removed, and exposed original plaster consolidated with dilute applications of acrylic resin. The edges of each section were carefully excavated by chisel and scalpel, and cleaned to the original surface plane. Old, non-historic surface coatings, were removed, and surface losses filled with plaster and textured to integrate them with the original art-work. When possible, old fill material covering

Dismantling of the Shaw Memorial, August 1996 by Daedalus, Inc.

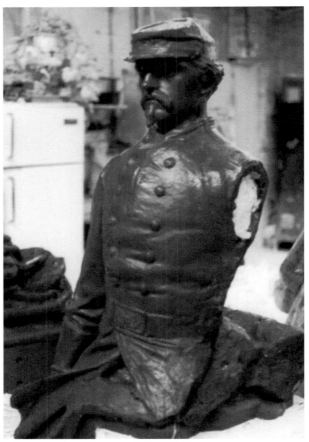

Wax figure of Shaw in preparation for bronze casting.

Three soldier sections with cleaned and prepared edges.

the original surface of the sections at the joint lines, was also removed. However, major areas of overfill were present along join lines in the section of the angel relief and in the base, to compensate for the misalignment and forward tilt of the horse. When conservators began to remove this overfill, they found that the original plaster was very abraded, had little or no surface detail, and in some cases, was scored to help attach new plaster skim coats added by Mr. Terken. In these areas, the decision was made to leave the old restoration plaster in place. Cracked and flaking areas were stabilized, and the entire surface was consolidated with Acryloid B-72 followed by Acryloid B-67 and two coats of wax in preparation for mold-making. The completed sections were shipped to Woburn, Massachusetts, for mold-making by Robert Shure of Skylight Studios, Inc.

Mold-Making

The considerable expertise of Robert Shure was absolutely essential throughout the entire project, during which he served as an invaluable link between conservation concerns and the realities of the casting process. Mr. Shure made frequent trips to the Modern Art Foundry to inspect the wax sections before enclosure in investment molds and the final casting in bronze by the lost-wax method. He consulted with the foundry on all aspects of assembly and final finishing.

Mold-making of the component sections was extremely challenging because of deep undercuts and areas of high relief. Because of the status of the plaster as an original artwork, it was not possible to cut the plaster sculpture into functional pieces for the bronze casting process. For example, in terms of mold-making, the section containing the drummer's hands, drumsticks, and straps holding the drum was perhaps the most complex area of the entire sculpture, required fifteen separate mold sections to faithfully capture these three-dimensional features. Registration or rotation marks were made in wax on the wrist of the soldier for incorporation in the rubber mold marking the correct attachment angle of the hand for the foundry's reference.

The back end of the horse was another challenging feature because the tail wraps around the proper left leg. The tail could not be removed for separate molding, and was too close to the body of the horse at the base to permit application of molding rubber and a plaster jacket, nor was there room enough to pull a rubber mold from the surface. In these and similar areas of the sculpture containing elements in the round or deeply undercut areas, gates or webs of unsulphonated, oil-based clay were placed in undercuts to contain the liquid molding rubber. A plaster cast was then made of the assembled part molds and trimmed of gates and webs with reference to the original artwork. The trimmed plaster cast was then cut into logical pieces for investing and pouring by the foundry.

Preparing mold of base

A combination of mold rubbers was used according to the surface features of individual sections. Black polysulphide rubber is the most flexible material, and was used for delicate detailed areas because it is easier to

Plaster cast from part molds of drummer boy hand detail

pull from complex surfaces. Polyurethane, a stiffer molding rubber, was used in larger, smoother areas like the horse's neck, head and flanks, where a less flexible rubber that would hold its shape was needed. Two coats of Butchers Wax™ were applied to the conserved and consolidated plaster surface as a release agent for the mold rubbers. The wax coatings and the layer of Acryloid B-67 were removed after the molds were completed.

Preparation for exhibit in the National Gallery of Art

Because most of the damage to the Shaw over time was the result of repeated installations, a significant part of the conservation project was the development of an armature system that will permit disassembly with the least possible impact on the integrity of the sculpture. This entails a design system for separate support of individual sections within an encompassing framework. Such a design was developed by the Daedalus, Inc. and was an integral part of the installation in the National Gallery of Art.

*Bronze cast being prepared at the
Modern Art Foundry, April 1997.*

*Drummer boy group showing
clean section edge.*

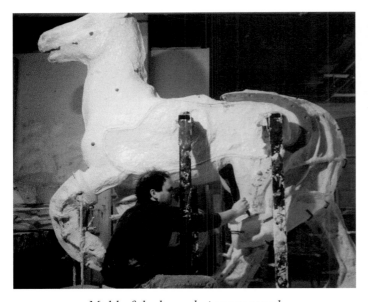

Mold of the horse being prepared.

ACKNOWLEDGEMENTS

We are indebted to the following scientists and conservators who contributed substantially toward the present conservation project of the Shaw Memorial:

Conservation Scientists

Richard Newman
Department of Objects Conservation and Scientific Research
Museum of Fine Arts, Boston

1997—Reflected Light Microscopy, FTIR microspectrometry, GC/MS and Electron Microprobe analysis of surface samples. *Museum of Fine Arts, Boston*

1981—Reflected Light and Polarized Light Microscopy, and SEM analyses with x-ray spectrometer of surface samples. *With Eugene Farrel, Center for Conservation and Technical Studies, Harvard University Museums.*

Michael Palmer
Conservation Division
Scientific Research Department
National Gallery of Art

1997—SEM/EDS analysis of surface samples. *National Gallery of Art*

Conservators

Carol Warner
National Park Service
Collections Conservation Branch
Northeast Cultural Resources Center

Shelley Sturman
Conservation Division
National Gallery of Art

Henry Lie
Center for Conservation and Technical Studies
Harvard University Museums.
Special thanks are extended to Arthur Beale of the Museum of Fine Arts for his long, valuable involvement and dedicated advocacy for the conservation of the Shaw Memorial since 1967, when, as a staff member of the Fogg Museum Center for Conservation and Technical Studies, he first recommended preservation measures in a General Collection Survey of Saint-Gaudens National Historic Site.

ENDNOTES

1. Craine, Clifford, "Recommendations for the Long Term Preservation of the Shaw Memorial Plaster at Saint-Gaudens NHS," Daedalus, Inc., Cambridge, Massachusetts, April 8, 1995
2. Museum Archives, The Museum of Fine Arts, Boston, Massachusetts. Saint-Gaudens arranged with the Director, Mr. Loring, to have "Chico," the museum's packer, go to the sculptor's New York studio in December, 1897, to pack and ship the Shaw cast to Paris.
3. Dartmouth College, Hanover, New Hampshire, Special Collections, *The Papers of Augustus Saint-Gaudens,* "Reminiscences of Augustus Saint-Gaudens," by William A. Coffin.
4. Schlesinger Library, Radcliffe College, Cambridge, Massachusetts, *Emerson-Nichols Papers,* Letter from Elisabeth Nichols to a relative, May 8, 1900
5. Dartmouth, Letter from William A. Coffin to Augustus Saint-Gaudens, October 19, 1901
6. Ibid, Letter from Edward B. Green to Augustus Saint-Gaudens, March 15, 1905
7. Ibid., Letter from Augustus Saint-Gaudens to Edward B. Green, July 4, 1905
8. Cornish, N.H., Saint-Gaudens National Historic Site, museum archives. Letter from John Terken to James W. Coleman, Jr., September 18, 1969.
9. Dartmouth, "Reminiscences of Augustus Saint-Gaudens," by William A. Coffin
10. Hoffman, Ethel, "At 73, He's Taken Apart His Pan American Jigsaw," *Buffalo Evening News,* March 26, 1949

INSCRIPTIONS ON
THE SHAW MEMORIAL IN BOSTON

In the field of the relief is inscribed the motto of the Society of the Cincinnati:

OMNIA RELINQVIT / SERVARE REMPVBLICAM

Below the relief on the front of the pedestal:

ROBERT GOULD SHAW
COLONEL·OF·THE·FIFTY·FOURTH·REGIMENT·OF MASSACHUSETTS·
INFANTRY·BORN·IN·BOSTON·10·OCTOBER·MDCCCXXXVII·
KILLED·WHILE·LEADING·THE·ASSAULT·ON·FORT·WAGNER·
SOUTH·CAROLINA·18·JULY·MDCCCLXIII

Underneath, the verse of James Russel Lowell:

RIGHT·IN·THE·VAN·ON·THE·RED·RAMPART'S·SLIPPERY· SWELL·
WITH·HEART·THAT·BEAT·A·CHARGE·HE·FELL·
FORWARD·AS·FITS·A·MAN:
BUT·THE·HIGH·SOUL·BURNS·ON·TO·LIGHT·MEN'S·FEET·
WHERE·DEATH·FOR·NOBLE· ENDS·MAKES·DYING·SWEET

TO THE FIFTY FOURTH
OF MASSACHUSETTS
REGIMENT INFANTRY

THE WHITE OFFICERS / TAKING LIFE AND HONOR
IN THEIR HANDS CAST IN THEIR LOT WITH MEN OF
A DESPISED RACE UNPROVED IN WAR AND RISKED
DEATH AS INCITERS OF SERVILE INSURRECTION IF
TAKEN PRISONERS BESIDES ENCOUNTERING ALL
THE COMMON
PERILS OF CAMP MARCH AND BATTLE

THE BLACK RANK AND FILE VOLUNTEERED WHEN
DISASTER CLOUDED THE UNION CAUSE SERVED
WITHOUT PAY FOR EIGHTEEN MONTHS TILL GIVEN
THAT OF WHITE TROOPS FACED THREATENED
ENSLAVEMENT IF CAPTURED WERE BRAVE IN
ACTION PATIENT UNDER HEAVY AND DANGEROUS
LABORS AND CHEERFUL AMID
HARDSHIPS AND PRIVATIONS

TOGETHER
THEY GAVE TO THE NATION AND THE WORLD
UNDYING PROOF THAT AMERICANS OF AFRICAN
DESCENT POSSESS THE PRIDE COURAGE
AND DEVOTION OF THE PATRIOT SOLDIER
ONE HUNDRED AND EIGHTY THOUSAND SUCH
AMERICANS ENLISTED UNDER THE UNION FLAG IN
MDCCCLXIII - MDCCCLXV

Below on the back, inscribed in 1897, are the names of the other five officers killed in battle. [Of these, only Russel and Simpkins died at Fort Wagner.]

CABOT JACKSON RUSSEL
CAPTAIN

WILLIAM HARRIS SIMPKINS
CAPTAIN

EDWARD LEWIS STEVENS
1ST LIEUTENANT

DAVID REID
1ST LIEUTENANT

FREDERICK HEDGE WEBSTER
2ND LIEUTENANT

Underneath these is an extract from the address given by Governor John A. Andrew on the departure of the regiment on May 28, 1863:

I KNOW NOT MR COMMANDER WHERE
IN ALL HUMAN HISTORY TO ANY
GIVEN THOUSAND MEN IN ARMS THERE
HAS BEEN COMMITTED A WORK AT
ONCE SO PROUD SO PRECIOUS SO FULL OF
HOPE AND GLORY AS THE
WORK COMMITTED TO YOU

On the marble at one end of the terrace are the words of the poet Anna Quincy Waterston:

O FAIR HAIRED NORTHERN HERO WITH
THY GUARD OF DUSKY HUE
UP FROM THE FIELD OF BATTLE RISE
TO THE LAST REVIEW

On the marble at the other end of the terrace are the words of the poet Ralph Waldo Emerson:

STAINLESS SOLDIER ON THE WALLS
KNOWING THIS AND KNOWS NO MORE
WHOEVER FIGHTS WHOEVER FALLS
JUSTICE CONQUERS EVERMORE

Booker T. Washington (1856-1915)

ADDRESS OF
BOOKER T. WASHINGTON

At the unveiling ceremony for the Shaw Memorial,
Music Hall, Boston, May 31, 1897

Mr. Chairman, and Fellow-Citizens: In this presence, and on this sacred and memorable day, in the deeds and death of our hero, we recall the old, old story, ever old, yet ever new, that when it was the will of the Father to lift humanity out of wretchedness and bondage, the precious task was delegated to him who among ten thousand was altogether lovely, and was willing to make himself of no reputation that he might save and lift up others.

If that heart could throb and if those lips could speak, what would be the sentiment and words that Robert Gould Shaw would have us feel and speak at this hour? He would not have us dwell long on the mistakes, the injustice, the criticisms of the days

> "Of storm and cloud, of doubt and fears
> Across the eternal sky must lower
> Before the glorious noon appears."

He would have us bind up with his own undying fame and memory, and retain by the side of his monument, the name of John A. Andrew, who, with prophetic vision and strong arm helped make the existence of the 54th Regiment possible; and that of George L. Stearns, who, with hidden generosity and a great sweet heart, helped to turn the darkest hour into day, and in doing so freely gave service, fortune, and life itself to the cause which this day commemorates. Nor would he have us forget those brother officers, living and dead, who, by their baptism in blood and fire, in defense of union and freedom, gave us an example of the highest and purest patriotism.

To you who fought so valiantly in the ranks, the scarred and scattered remnant of the 54th Regiment, who with empty sleeve and wanting leg have honored this occasion with your presence,—to you your commander is not dead. Though Boston erected no monument, and history recorded no story, in you and the loyal race which you represent, Robert Gould Shaw would have a monument which time could not wear away.

But an occasion like this is too great, too sacred, for mere individual eulogy. The individual is the instrument, national virtue the end. That which was three hundred years being woven into the warp and woof of our democratic institutions could not be effaced by a single battle, as magnificent as was that battle; that which for three centuries had bound master and slave, yea, North and South, to a body of death, could not be blotted out by four years of war, could not be atoned for by shot and sword, nor by blood and tears.

Not many days ago, in the heart of the South, in a large gathering of the people of my race, there were heard from many lips praises and thanksgiving to God for his goodness in setting them free from physical slavery. In the midst of that assembly a

Southern white man arose, with gray hair and trembling hands, the former owner of many slaves, and from his quivering lips there came the words: "My friends, you forget in your rejoicing that in setting you free God was also good to me and my race in setting us free." But there is a higher and deeper sense in which both races must be free than that represented by the bill of sale. The black man who cannot let love and sympathy go out to the white man is but half free. The white man who would close the shop or factory against a black man seeking an opportunity to earn an honest living is but half free. The white man who retards his own development by opposing a black man is but half free. The full measure of the fruit of Fort Wagner and all that this monument stands for will not be realized until every man covered by a black skin shall, by patience and natural effort, grow to that height in industry, property, intelligence, and moral responsibility, where no man in all our land will be tempted to degrade himself by withholding from his black brother any opportunity which he himself would possess.

Until that time comes, this monument will stand for effort, not victory complete. What these heroic souls of the 54th Regiment began, we must complete. It must be completed not in malice, nor narrowness, nor artificial progress, nor in efforts at mere temporary political gain, nor in abuse of another section or race. Standing as I do to-day in the home of Garrison and Phillips and Sumner, my heart goes out to those who wore the gray as well as to those clothed in blue, to those who returned defeated to destitute homes, to face blasted hopes and shattered political and industrial system. To them there can be no prouder reward for defeat than by a supreme effort to place the Negro on that footing where he will add material, intellectual, and civil strength to every department of state.

This work must be completed in public school, industrial school, and college. The most of it must be completed in the effort of the Negro himself; in his effort to withstand temptation, to economize, to exercise thrift, to disregard the superficial for the real, the shadow for the substance, to be great and yet small; in his effort to be patient in the laying of a firm foundation, to so grow in skill and knowledge that he shall place his services in demand by reason of his intrinsic and superior worth. This, this is the key that unlocks every door of opportunity, and all others fail. In this battle of peace, the rich and poor, the black and white may have a part.

What lesson has this occasion for the future? What of hope, what of encouragement, what of caution? "Watchman, tell us of the night, what the signs of promise are." If through me, an humble representative, nearly ten millions of my people might be permitted to send a message to Massachusetts, to the survivors of the 54th Regiment, to the committee whose untiring energy has made this memorial possible, to the family who gave their only boy that we might have life more abundantly, that message would be: Tell them that the sacrifice was not in vain, that up from the depths of ignorance and poverty we are coming, and if we come through oppression, out of the struggle we are gaining strength; by way of the school, the well-cultivated field, the skilled hand, the Christian home, we are coming up; that we propose to invite all who will to step up and occupy this position with us. Tell them that we are learning that standing ground for a race, as for an individual, must be laid in intelligence, industry, thrift, and property, not as an end, but as a means to the highest privileges; that we are learning that neither the conqueror's bullet, nor fiat of law, could make an ignorant voter an intelligent voter, could make a dependent man an independent man, could give one citizen respect for another, a bank account, a foot of land, or an enlightened fireside. Tell them that, as grateful as we are to artist and patriotism for placing the figures of Shaw and his comrades in physical form of beauty and magnificence, that after all the real monument, the greater monument, is being slowly but safely builded among the lowly in the South, in the struggles and sacrifices of a race to justify all that has been done and suffered for it.

One of the wishes that lay nearest to Colonel Shaw's heart was, that his black troops might be permitted to fight by the side of white soldiers. Have we not lived to see that wish realized, and will it not be more so in the future? Not at Wagner, not with rifle and bayonet, but on the field of peace, in the battle of industry, in the struggle for good government, in the lifting up of the lowest to the fullest opportunities. In this we shall fight by the side of white men North and South. And if this be true, as under God's guidance it will, that old flag, that emblem of progress and security which brave Sergeant Carney never permitted to fall upon the ground, will still be borne aloft by Southern soldier and Northern soldier, and in a more potent and higher sense we shall all realize that

" The slave's chain and the master's
Alike are broken.
The one curse of the races
Held both in tether:
They are rising,—all are rising,
The black and white together! "

ADDITIONAL NAMES

In 1981, the Shaw Memorial in Boston was restored. The following names of the enlisted men of the Fifty-Fourth killed in action during the war were added to the monument.

THE MEMORY OF THE JUST IS BLESSED

Henry Albert

Thomas R. Ampey

Thomas Bowman

William Brady

Abraham Brown

James H. Buchanan

Henry F. Burghardt

Elisha Burkett

Jason Champlin

Andrew Clark

Lewis Clark

Henry Craig

Josephus Curry

Edward Darks

Henry Dennis

William Edgerly

Albert Evans

William S. Everson

Samuel Ford

Richard M. Foster

Charles S. Gamrell

Lewis C. Green

John Hall

William Henry Harrison, II

Edward Hines

Benjamin Hogan

Charles M. Holloway

George Jackson

James P. Johns

John H. Johnson

Daniel A. Kelley

Henry King

Cyrus Krunkleton

Augustus Lewis

Thomas Lloyd

William Lloyd

Lewis J. Locard

Francis Lowe

Robert McJohnson

John Miller

James H. Mills

William H. Morris

Charles E. Nelson

Stephen Newton

Harrison Pierce

Cornelius Price

Thomas Peter Riggs

David R. Roper

Anthony Schenck

Thomas Sheldon

William J. Smith

Samuel Sufshay

John Tanner

William Thomas

Charles Van Allen

George Vanderpool

Cornelius Watson

Edward Williams

Franklin Willis

Joseph D. Wilson

William Wilson

John W. Winslow

Author's note: These names did not include those who died of their wounds, died in prison camps, died of disease, or were listed as missing after a battle. A complete roster of the Fifty-Fourth Regiment may be found in *History of the Fifty-Fourth Regiment of Massachusetts Volunteer Infantry, 1863-1865*, by Capt. Luis Emilio.

1997
BOARD OF TRUSTEES OF THE SAINT-GAUDENS MEMORIAL

INDEX

THE SHAW MEMORIAL
A CELEBRATION OF AN AMERICAN MASTERPIECE

Designed and composed by Barbara Jones
in Mrs. Eaves, Adobe typeface
with display lines in Diotoma Adobe typeface.
Printed at The Pond-Ekberg Company, Chicopee, Massachusetts.

Photo credits:
Lyle Peterville, p. 23 and pages in color section, heads and details.
Jeffrey Nintzel, p. 53, 61, 108
Gregory C. Schwarz, p. 31, 62, new bronze cast in color section
Carol Warner, p. 109-112